The Undiscovered Abode

The Undiscovered Abode

A deep insight into the psychology of human beings, and an attempt to search solutions to the challenges of human life from within

Geetika Bhardwaj

GenNext Publication

First Published, 2019

Published by

GenNext Publication
5, Ansari Road
Daryaganj, New Delhi-110002
Phone: 9811692060
E-mail: gennextpublication@hotmail.com

Printed at: G. Print Process, Delhi.

Cataloging in Publication Data—DK
Courtesy: D.K. Agencies (P) Ltd. <docinfo@dkagencies.com>

Bhardwaj, Geetika, author.
The undiscovered abode: a deep insight into the psychology of human beings, and an attempt to search solutions to the challenges of human life from within / Geetika Bhardwaj.
pages cm
ISBN 9789380223506

1. Conduct of life. 2. Self-actualization (Psychology) I. Title.

LCC BJ1589.B43 2019 | DDC 158.1 23

The book is dedicated to my sister Rachita Sharma who has been a major contributor to the writing of this book. She has not only inspired me morally but has also motivated me at times when rough and uneven terrains made the trail of life tough for me. Currently, she is in Sydney, Australia. I wish her all luck and success in her future endeavors!

Contents

Preface

Life................, is a puzzle for most of the people. Some would like to describe it in the simplest way, e.g. life is a journey full of struggles. Others would like to decipher their thoughts in weird ways. But all will agree with a fact that no one is being able to define life completely. There are few people who have reached and understood the depth of life. That depth is an approximately indefinable sphere towards which the wheel of life moves and it moves at a faster pace for the real deservers and searchers.

But why are we discussing the depth of life must be an apparent question in your minds. It's for the sake of finding solutions to the enormous puzzles related to our lives. You must have read many books on life, spirituality, the purpose of life, how to lead a good life. Don't worry; neither am I going to repeat the same things nor am I boasting of feeding you with everything new. But I can assure that you will not mind spending time after reading a few pages, and may think on the completion this book that it was worth reading.

To tell you frankly, the puzzles of our lives are like our relatives which keep us busy throughout our lifetimes. Everyone everywhere on this earth is thinking of his life's one or another puzzle. The first thing which should be the aftermath of reading this first page is that all of us should try taking these puzzles as life's challenges for us to resolve. Sounds unrealistic, isn't it? Yes, it can happen!

Try to adopt a less negative or rather a positive outlook towards them. If we welcome a thing with a negative outlook, somehow it will be linked to the thread of negativity throughout. Welcoming a thing with positive outlook, results in a positive energy level in the person, thus providing him all the armour for fighting the negativity that surrounds his life. In this whole process, some important elements are involved. Before moving further towards the details of puzzles found in our lives, we should be well aware of the concept of life. I am using the word concept as life can never be tied in words, which are so insufficient and incompetent so as to define life.

Life is neither tangible nor completely intangible. It is not like materialistic possessions like luxury goods but one can possess it and keep it in one's heart. Hence it is valuable. It is an asset. It is not tangible as one can't feel it by the touch of hand. Although, it is not completely intangible as it can be touched by one's heart and touches one's heart too. Life has properties more like water which is ever flowing, taking the form of the vessel in which it is put, having the same colors as of the liquid in which it is mixed, has oxygen that is invaluable for living beings.

Hence resemblance of life and water is apparent. I would like to say here that fluid nature of life envelops all other manifestations of it for life never stops and in moving from one shore to another it gathers various properties too. "Life is a great or the greatest teacher", everyone says. Life is a great student too, that I firmly believe in. What we will teach life in the beginning years, it will never forget, memorize it, and will form values, ideals, morals and fundamentals based on it. This student has one special quality that it comes to us with its querries, tells us what is going wrong and the one who wants to change for the better can take hints from this meticulous student's work. The sphere of life is very large and one can talk endlessly about it.

Well, before we have our share of serious talk about life, there are certain fundamentals which have to be cleared. It is almost the same thing that without learning how to walk, a young child cannot run or without learning the basic chapter of the English Alphabet in school, a child will not be able to master the language or speak it fluently either. Hence without wasting much of your precious time and energy, I would like to proceed.

But before that, I would love all of you to ponder over life as reflected in my wordings of the poem given on the next page.

E-Mail: geetika10.2013@gmail.com

"Oh Life! Why are you so complicated and ever-changing?
Oh Life! Why are you always busy like a bee and ever-engaging?
Life! I do love you but with hesitations and restrictions;
Life! I do want to have a longer inning with a lot of possessions.
Life! You, you are not real, are you? Are you not imaginary?
Where my mind dwells & which suits my heart, you are that scenery!
Life, are you my love or are you my love of this world?
Do I truly value you or in the unrealistic sphere, am I held?
Life! I cannot see you, still I see through your eyes;
Oh Dear! I cannot touch you; still I feel life in every touch.
Did you ever call me Life or have I always ignored your just voice;
Is it not true that you always guided correct, I still made wrong choice.
Life! You are the shadow which never left me alone in the universe;
It is only me who ditched you, blamed you as destiny, as a curse.
You are that unheard song of my heart which belongs only to me;
You give me shadow, fruits of wisdom, you are the divine tree.
You being a true lover always gave cushion of support to my heart;
You made me feel complete; you are the whole, not a single part.
Do you realize how many times did I let you down?
By being angry, self-rejective and with my face with frown!
People say that Life is a treasure; I say you are simply immense;
Holds us all, our feelings, tolerates everything being intense!
Oh Life! You have guts, I must say! We can learn courage from you;
Fall, Be defeated, destroyed & rise up once again as we can do it too!
You are a freaky teacher who knows all and when to teach what?
You know well when to supply energy & power, when to cut!
Care & precaution is what you teach slowly & towards the other edge;
We gain knowledge, become wise and not to err, we pledge!
Life! Oh My Dear! I love you with and without all reasons;
I will live for you and die for you all seasons!"

Acknowledgement

Although the writing of this book is my individual effort but the there are scenarios which are not apparent but are vital to the writing of any book or behind any creative task. An individual has the power within to initiate a task, to make true-hearted and genuine efforts for a task at hand, but the task is fully accomplished by the combined efforts of all, including family, friends, acquaintances, and well-wishers.

While writing this book, my first inspiration comes from my sister who has always encouraged me and has motivated me to the extent that this book has now become a reality. It was her dream that my ideas must be compiled and brought forward. Not only this, she believes that it is for the benefit of all. It is her view that if anyone can benefit a larger number of people by his effort, then that person must work in the right direction and put all his efforts towards the achievement of such noble goal.

She is another one except my father who has patiently listened to all my ideas. She has provided me moral support while I dedicated myself to writing this book. She has lent me her hand in the darker period of my life. Her shoulder is one such place in the world on which I can take rest in my morose mood. She is the possessor of such a loving and supportive heart that she has always helped people around her in times of need including me. People like her are rare and precious for this earth and God. At the beginning stage, she used to practice meditation and read books related to spirituality. Then, I gained interest in these things and it grew with the passing time. The time came when I felt one with the Almighty.

I would not tell a lie that since my childhood, I have been a person who believed in meditation and spirituality. Although I have been an avid reader since the beginning, yet I used to read course books, some good story books, current affair magazines, and some general books. It was Rachita who bought me nearer to God. With time, I realized that such things relate us to the inner self and in the long run, it provides us with all the solutions to the challenges of life.

There are a few other people who have motivated me a lot towards the writing of this book and wanted to see the accomplishment of this task. One of such persons was my maternal grandfather, Mr. SomDutt Sharma. He has always inspired me and wanted to see me achieve great heights. It is unfortunate that we lost him in the year 2011. He was the national secretary of Boys Scouts Association and always used to write in the scouter regularly. He won National Award for scouts, The Silver Elephant too. He used to say that if one never loses the will power to achieve a goal, then no defeat is final. Hismemories are still fresh in my mindand can never fade away. He was a man of high morals and values and expected the same from junior members of his family. To find such a torchbearer andinspirational light in today's era is rare.

My third major and infinite source of motivation is my parents. There are parents in the world who expect everything from their children but cannot provide the children a patient ear. There used to be times when there was dark at night and I used to wake them up to read and listen what I have written. They have always lent me a patient ear. They are the kind of parents who tolerate to the extreme level to see the potential in their child grow. They have provided us with the amenities they could and more than that they have taught us to be morally right, to follow the correct path, be it longer or full of losses, and have nurtured in us the value of education.

I would like to thank my husband who has always been with me through thick and thin. He believes that if I have capability to put my ideas on paper and in case, they are of good use to others, I must do so. He even after his hectic daily schedule listens to what I have written and always motivates me. Similarly, my father-in-law too have always encouraged me and believes that good writing can change the attitude of people. He even says that I can delay any household work but should prioritize my writing work. Last but not the least; I would like to thank God who has given me right attitude and framework of mind which helped me a lot in my journey. God has always been kind to me in many ways and has blessed me with a loving and passionate family, good and dependable friends and has provided me the opportunity to meet many people in my life who have guided me through.

I thank all these people from the depth of my heart and pay my gratitude to all of these. May God give them all the success and prosperity in life!

Chapter - 1

The Basic Concept of Puzzles

Life has diversities which are visible everywhere. Diversity is an important constituent of life without which life is colorless and like a fragrance-less flower. We can see different folks busy in different jobs, some wealthy, some middle class, and some who are always busy in earning their one square meal a day.

And there are other diversities too like the diversities in interpreting others, diversities in nature, diversities in culture, and diversities in ways of living. Life is full of cheer and blues. It has a lot to give us and we can explore a lot in the form of achievements. They come with wonder and fill our hearts with passion, affection and leave us embezzled.

Someone may feel that he has not achieved anything in life or has achieved less or small. But such person should always think that God has blessed him with life which in itself a priceless and incomparable achievement. Achievements appearing big usually give us a number of small dissatisfactions and regrets on entering our lives. Beauty of living life is enjoying every second to its fullest. One should try to give one's best to the precious time given by the God and simultaneously live with zeal and vigor, enjoying the fragrance of the flower of life.

So did you notice the fact that life is full of extremes too? Such are the extremes of life that on the one hand someone is worried about the turnover of his company and on the other hand another person in another corner is worried about the one square meal for him and his family. On the one hand a person is enjoying sleep in his luxurious house and on the other side; a family is sleeping on the pavement in one of the coldest nights of winter. Two children are of the same age group but one goes to school and the other picks up the rags in front of the same school. Two girls of the same age, of whom one can dream of her nice future and the other due to circumstances has to bear the burden of a family and work day & night for the other siblings and parents. So, there are a lot of problems in this world.

We were talking about the puzzles of life and I don't think that there is any puzzle bigger than the one that why such big extremes occur in our world? Why don't these inequalities vanish? I hope that if we think deeply about it, we will feel lightened for sometime as our puzzles are not greater than the described one. But I completely agree with the fact that when one is surrounded by a problem or is facing a serious puzzle of one's life, nothing can easily pacify him.

Life takes a person to various destinations and one has to cover different paths to reach them. In the gap between the starting point and the destination, that path puts forth various puzzles in front of us in the form of tough situations. There is no denying the fact that testing times come in everyone's life. But one need not lose strength and hope.

Hardship or adversity teaches us a lot in life. It teaches us the value of life, the value of time, how to develop a strong will power and enhances our confidence level. The person who has faced adversity comes out as a winner in life and emerges as an altogether different person. That person who has faced adversity is a winner in his own eyes which is one of the most satisfying attributes of adversity. So, one should take the testing times sportingly and take them as opportunities to prove his real worth as it is only under adverse conditions that the strength and wisdom of a person are truly tested. I am denoting these tough times as puzzles of life as it is only under these conditions that a person feels exhausted of life, weak and puzzled and mostly no solution comes to his mind at first.

Sometimes it gives us a chance to prepare ourselves for that situation and sometimes the throw of the hidden surprise is so sudden and fast that we are caught unaware. It depends solely on two major factors that how well a puzzle can be resolved: one being the situation and the other being the capacity of a person to handle it.

Situations facing a person can be of many types, viz, a tricky situation needing the application of brain and which can be solved by proper reasoning and logic, situations which are tough but require more patience and can be solved by the use of a cool mind and there are situations which require quick decisions to be taken and thus require fast decision making capability. There can be another classification of situations like personal situations, professional situations and others. And we should realize the fact that everyone has the capacity to handle difficult situations, some have more while others have less. But one can develop or increase the potential to fight the odd situations in one's life by focusing on the aim, analyzing the situation correctly and then solving the problem with a cool, calm, and composed mind. Whenever faced with a problem, we should always behave in a balanced manner lest everything may result in chaos.

So, man has been provided with all the armaments for fighting in life and these weapons include patience, intellect, the power to focus on something, the potential to do hard work, the capability of innovation and thus creating something new, strong will power and the strength of determination. So we should never forget that if the problem faced by us is big, then we are also well-equipped to face it like a prince. We should never belittle ourselves and must do justice to the abilities gifted to us by the Almighty.

By the time, we have a clear picture of life's puzzles in our minds. Although we have so far discussed the nature of situations in life, yet we have still much to discover more about it. One thing is for sure that a person who faces any kind of difficulty in life with courage wins half of the battle as any battle fought with courage and confidence is half won. When faced with a personal challenge, one should be patient and caring as relations are involved in it.

When a challenge encounters you on professional front, you should deal with it with tact, diplomacy, reason and logic as nobody is concerned with your emotional front. In case you are faced with an emotional challenge, then first you need to be cool & calm and then try to pacify yourself using your intellect too. In this matter you may need to take the help of a dear one as when one is emotionally trapped, he is not being able to properly use his other powers. Nowadays, societal problems are also raising their heads and one needs to be very strong in order to face them. If we look at the problems superficially, they all will appear to be similar but all of them are different from one another and in the same way, the methods of solving them differ from each other.

Life not always glows; we may face the blues;
But we should be aware of all the clues;
That tells us how to reach the top horizon;
And we should apply the most powerful weapon;
That is gifted to us by the Almighty;
That is our brain and brings us all the gaiety!

Chapter - 2

Various Goals in Life

Everyone in this world has goals which vary from person to person. Goals may be small and they may be big too but they have an important position in one's life. If a person's life is lacking goal, then the life almost becomes meaningless and the heart of the person is filled with the feeling of idleness. For gaining prosperity in life, it is indispensable that one has the enthusiasm of doing something worthwhile in life which happens only if a person has a set goal in his mind. So, we will be dealing with various types of goals in this chapter in detail.

Different people have varied goals. Goals are broadly classified into personal goals, materialistic goals, and spiritual goals. Personal goals further include academic goals, professional goals, marital goals, emotional goals. Materialistic goals include career goals, wealth gaining goals, power goals, and others depending upon individuals. Spiritual goals are also there but are rarely longed for.

Academic goals are person specific. They can also be called career goals. Thus, such types of goals come under both the categories, personal goals and materialistic goals. The selection of academia mostly affects the career in future. Career goals are chosen by various people according to their academia, working potentials, intellects and growth expectations. Sometimes career choices are modified due to constraints like time, money, environmental factors and health. Most of the folks remain confused in career selection and hence create fuss and havoc in their own lives and simultaneously those who are concerned feel burdened. Children should be given the freedom to choose their respective careers as they are the only ones who know their interests better. Whether we talk of parents or teachers, both of them have a long-term view of a child's future. Somewhere, somehow, in this complete process of care, the basic interests of children remain hidden. Need today is to explore such interests and dreams attached to them and we will be able to see a much better tomorrow. Expecting too much from a child usually leads to disturbances in a child's life, creates confusion in his mind regarding his studies and some other things. A sensitive child may like to fulfill his parents' dreams and go accordingly whereas on the other hand another child may adopt a stubborn attitude and would like to go for his own dreams. The former kind of child may kill his original dreams and some belonging to this category may keep their dreams related to studies in their hearts forever and simultaneously heed parents' advice. The latter type of child struggles, fights for his right to choose his own career and can be more assertive and pressurizing as a child. Such children are more satisfied, happy and feel blessed at later stages of their lives.

Professional goals are included in the category of personal goals. There is a difference in career goals and professional goals. One can be in one profession at a time and can change that for deciding a full-time career later on. Career is a long-term phenomenon and to be successful in career one has to be well planned and move towards the decided direction. People choose professions according to varied factors like circumstances, financial needs, short-term goals, etc. Most of the people choose those professions which benefit them the most financially. Some go for stability, job-satisfaction, value in the organization, market value of the firm, etc. Some continue in the same profession and pursue it as a full-time career. Some others take a route through different professions and then arrive at a career for themselves.

Marital goals are also one of the personal goals which are least described but are as important as any other type of goal. Those who are not serious or prepared to marry, if get married may feel burdened later on. Psychologically getting prepared to marry is an essential ingredient of married life. Only when a mature individually is psychologically ready to marry, then should, plans be made for his or her marriage.

Some people remain confused in deciding when to marry while the others remain uncertain about the correct life-partner. One can spend the life with a person who is caring, understanding and financially independent. The presence of these three aspects ensures other things. Care breeds trust, understanding results in commitment and financial independence leads to a feeling security of a smooth life with your life partner. Male members of the society usually seek someone who can take the responsibility of the entire household and on whom all can rely.

Those who don't take such goals seriously find this as one of their biggest mistakes of life which affects the later stage of their lives. It is an occasion of divine grace when two people with a lot of communion tie the wedlock.

Emotional goals are also personal goals and are a commonly misunderstood concept. Usually, they are taken to be related to the person who is more emotional. If we realize, while being emotional we care more for the other person who may be a family member, guardian, teacher or a friend. The other person person involved becomes our center of focus and that is from where most of the challenges germinate. Then our heart dominates our reasoning and decision-making ability & sometimes overpowers the brain. I am describing emotions as goals as they are also directed towards special people.

Now we will be discussing materialistic goals. I am really not comfortable with the fact that in this age if one talks about materialism, why it is considered a taboo by some. If someone is less spiritual or not spiritual, then it is his specific choice to be so. Career goals are already described. In the long run, a good career gives a status hike which provides confidence to most of the people.

Wealth gaining goals are centuries old and not a new addition to the list of professional goals. Everybody to different extent wants to amass wealth. This is not a bad thing, for sure. Dear have you analyzed the time allocation and satisfaction levels attached to this specific category in your life? Everyone prefers to be financially secure, does many efforts towards the achievement of this. Perfectly fine, I agree with this. But trouble creeps in when we don't know how to maintain a balance between such goals and other indispensable things in our lives. I will not be repeating the same old-fashioned fact that there is no use of amassed wealth if there is no one left to share. Youth of today knows thousands of ways to spend money and they can guarantee their parents that if left alone they will get hundreds of friends who will accompany them. They are right at their own level as in this materialistic world everything seems to be so easy that their thinking has gone this way. For solving their simple problems, weird thoughts enter their minds. They are not to blame solely as they have adopted this from their homes and from the society. Coming back to our previous topic, wealth gained is good, in case it doesn't disturb our peace of minds which is a mutated child of inner satisfaction and healthy thinking. Sometimes we try a lot but are not able to maintain a proper balance between wealth gaining goals and other precious things in life. This is that time of our lives when, we, by using all our potential try to tread the path of a healthy life. This can be achieved by grit, determination, will power, good confidence level and of course a healthy thinking. The balance, thus achieved is due to our effort and pleasure thus gained is everlasting. Pleasure got by struggling in our lives and overcoming those struggles, remains in our hearts forever like evergreen leaves. It spreads such everlasting fragrance in our lives which is incomparable, rejuvenating and re-energizing.

Power goals are also an inseparable part of materialistic goals. The difference lies in the fact that some people strive for one kind of power and others strive for other kind. Another major aspect is that some folks are transparent enough to mention their intentions while others have hidden desires.

Power has many colors and is of various kinds like spiritual power, divine power, monitory power, authoritative power, legal powers, moral power, power of knowledge, and brain prowess. Although spiritual and divine powers sound very similar yet are different in nature and perspective. One is treading the path to God with full dedication and devotion while the other is the feeling we have on meeting the Creator of this whole world. In the former case, we get some spiritual powers and in the latter case, we experience some special powers called divine powers. There is a divine rule which governs the usage of these powers which says that the person possessing these powers cannot use them for negative motives.

Some people have some other goals or destinations to reach in life. Some would like to render their services to the society and some would like to work for enhancing their own spiritual and divine capabilities. Getting satisfaction through watching others work efficiently who were otherwise unable to work properly or compete with others, is a soulful thing. Lack of self-confidence or the feeling of being dependent is a silent killer. This is something which cannot be shared with everyone. Understanding such dearth of security and confidence and helping that person indirectly is a tough task. A person with the right attitude towards service of mankind and with the right appetite for solving such hidden challenges behind otherwise smiling faces can perform this social duty.

The hunger should be there to see someone in distress smiling, to see a crying face healed, to see a broken heart rejuvenated, to feel a traumatized soul in peace, to create a love niche for all, to assemble tits and bits of care & peace for forming a safe nest for all. Spiritual and divine goals give a person greater responsibilities than other human beings.

In short, there are numerous other kinds of goals or ambitions which have not been described under these categories. Goals are person-specific. Ambitions are an individualistic issue. There can be as many numbers of ambitions as there are people on this planet. The basic thing is how one reaches a goal. If the journey to the destination has been tiresome, boring, or lengthy, it implies that either the goal was not of the choice of the particular person or the way adopted to achieve it; was wrong. Those who tread the path joyfully, find the journey soulful. Such people never think about the challenges of the path, bravely face every odd. Courage is the key to life's battle. The moment you achieve your aim, leaves you embezzled.

Those striving for satisfaction and harmony must tread the path of spirituality. The acquisition of satisfaction can be by various means. Most of the people try to derive satisfaction from materialistic possessions or by fulfillment of materialistic desires. It should also be viewed from an individualistic angle. Some search emotional satisfaction in personal relationships while few other rely on a broader picture of life for seeking satisfaction. Thus, the chart of satisfaction varies from person to person and has many ups and downs. Satisfaction can be momentary and satisfaction can be for lifetime too. Degrees do vary.

Spiritual satisfaction is a rare thing longed for by true searchers. Satisfaction is an attribute of the mind and the heart. It connects both and it liberates both. One has to dispense away the mental powers sometimes during spiritual practices as mind being capable of comprehending and analyzing may interfere with the union of the self with the Self. We usually live in outer self's sphere. But the need is to unite it with the inner Self, which is none else than the divine.

To be in nearly perfect harmony with the self, both the heart and the mind must correlate, coordinate, unite with the inner self, be one with the Divine and try to serve mankind. The beginners may come across obstacles like distractions, disinterest, deficit of devotion, decline of concentration level at occasions, but later on this way, one will find utmost satisfaction, tranquility and liberation.

Amidst increasing levels of ambitions, busy schedules, careless lifestyles, dastardly passions, emotional turmoil, fetch-up tendencies, grievances of varying degrees, hampering attitudes, the I-factor, juvenile tendencies, the Super Ego, Childish Ego and loads of other responsibilities, one has to maintain a good level of balance of mind and heart. Spiritual and divine goals are the pathways to achieve this.

Towards the achievement of this harmonious balance, one has to be determined to pursue the path of spirituality undeterred. I would not like to keep you in dark or give you false promises as the path of spirituality costs various things up to varying degrees. They include less desire for materialistic pursuits, least worldly bondages, and above them a soulful connection with the inner self. If one desires to achieve something, he must fix a goal in mind and set a deadline. Goal once fixed fills you with energy and enthusiasm that will lead you towards it. The path in between is difficult for those who try to overcome their obstacles taking them far more seriously. They unconsciously give more weight age to those obstacles instead of the goal. They invest a major chunk of their time resource in overcoming those obstacles. The path is easier for those who try to maintain a balance between overpowering their hurdles and achieving their goal. They spend their time in both these tasks equally.

There are no sharp peaks and no deadly lows in the voyage of life. Life contains vast diversity of challenges; amongst them are small or medium crests of little happiness gathered and small troughs of few lows coming our ways. Sometimes life has lot more to offer like a big opportunity coupled with a long-term odd, or a suitable change coupled with some uncertainties. Many things in life are like a mirage which can be seen, hoped for but can never be achieved. Such things just fill our hearts with momentary joy or pleasure.

Spiritual goals are rarely longed for and are known by the seeker only. Academic goals vary depending upon the intellect of people, study potential, resources available and the environment given. Those who have a zest for studies will always be focused determined and enjoy their studies. People choose their academic goals according to their interests but in reality they are a combined result of all the above mentioned factors.

Professional goals depending upon people are diverse. One enters a profession for financial and personal growth. Professionals always strive for good remuneration coupled with job satisfaction. Mostly healthy competition and work with dignity are loved. Marital goals are least defined and are at a low in one's priority list nowadays. But they are an important part of lives of many. The decline in the position of such goals in one's life is mainly due to the rising expectations of youngsters about their companions. Life can be smoothly and lovingly spent with a person who cares for you, loves you and is committed to you.

If such two people tie wedlock, then everything else is taken care of by life itself. Emotional goals are taken as related to one's own emotions but in reality you are caring for someone else more than you, be it your family members, friends or the beloved. Such goals are symbiotic and emotions are nurturing.

Emotions can be fatal if one expects much from the concerned person and as a result become too dependent on that person. In this case too, maintaining a proper balance between other aspects of life and emotions plays a major role in one's emotional life and life as a whole. Some realize that at a later stage being overemotional can cause hindrances in their growth as well as people also recognize that emotions may cast a negative shadow on the lives of their near and dear ones who are positively related to them and are worried about them. The sooner a person accepts this reality and starts acting proactively towards lessening of emotional dependence, maintaining a balance between positive and negative emotions, managing the emotions on a whole and works towards inculcating more, new and positive emotions, life will become a season of spring for him and others too. Like attracts like, hence positive emotions and thoughts will attract new, innovative, varied positive emotions and vibrant thoughts from the others in the surroundings. Hence, we come to a very simple conclusion here that that the secret to achieve a goal, whether big or small, is to take it seriously and put in all the hard work to accomplish that.

Challenges are a part and parcel of one's life;
In the beginning, may create some strife;
Later in the journey, they only help;
As they guide and teach us to discipline self;
They tell us that life has a lot more to give;
We have so many special moments to live;
But before that we have a test to pass;
Which all have to take and none can surpass;
It is a test of hard work and persistence;
It is indispensable for our sustenance;
It is lovingly called by us: challenges;
And beyond it our whole life scenario changes;
Come out of giggles and light laughs;
Challenges are our real better halves.

Chapter - 3

Types of Challenges

Life has many challenges, unfolded for us. It engulfs in itself, the surprises of life which are revealed with time. Although chronologically, we should have first discussed the types of life's challenges yet we have already discussed how to face those challenges. In this manner, one can easily decide how to deal with a particular type of challenge. Our minds are also free of apprehensions that come easily in the mind with the word challenge. There are various kinds of challenges involved in the process of our lives which are depicted as below:

(1) Basic challenges of life
(2) Challenges of the society
(3) Challenges of the marital life
(4) Emotional challenges
(5) Adaptability challenges
(6) Professional challenges
(7) Challenges of adolescent life
(8) Aging challenges
(9) Fitness challenges
(10) Challenges of love life

We will be taking the detailed description of all the challenges one by one and will have a close watch. It is as follows:-

1. Basic challenges of life:- Many challenges are related to the basic amenities of life. There are many people who are less privileged

and are deprived of things like food, clothing, shelter, education, health services and future security. If one is deprived of these basic needs of life, then it leads to chaos in his life and may lead to social unrest. These challenges are always dealt with at the priority basis as without facing them properly one cannot move further in life smoothly. One who is involved in facing these challenges rarely thinks of anything else. These are such hardships which should be dealt with strength of mind, body and soul. Many people in this world face these situations and fight day and night for achieving their aim of overcoming the respective situation. There is no specific solution for dealing with such challenges except that one should not lose hope. It always depends upon the situation which differs from person to person and it is also hard to empathize with the people who face such tough challenges in their lives. So, if you are not among that lot who is facing the basic challenges of life, you should feel blessed and thank God. We can contribute towards a better situation in their lives by practicing small things in our daily lives like the educated lot can teach the deprived children in their free time. There are many other contributions which we can make towards a better society.

2. Challenges of the society:- This category of challenges is a newly cropped up category and include the challenges one has to face in the society. These challenges include various kinds of insecurities one faces while living in the society, and various kinds of pressures from the society. Due to these challenges, many kinds of disorders are also spreading among the masses including hypertension, depression, high blood pressure, other kinds of brain disorders, and many kinds of other physical diseases too. If we talk with respect to the Indian society, it has its own positive and negative points but there are many pressures which have a negative impact on one's life. While dealing with such pressures, along with strong determination, tact and a strong will power, a very strong mind is also required. This strength of mind is a very important factor as the pressure may be direct or indirect and one must be fully prepared to face it.

The basic societal values are based on providing a feeling of security to every member of it, and respecting an individual's identity, his thoughts, dignity and emotions. But the radical change which the society of every nation is facing in general is all about conflicts of egos. There is a conflict between egos of two communities, castes, creeds, sections or individuals. All this has led to the demolition of the old structure of every society which paid attention towards group interests and interest of the nation too instead of prioritizing individual interests alone. Nowadays, the seeds of non-tolerance are being sown in the soil that germinates into a resulting crop of young people who hardly tolerate difference of opinion. There are a few people left with tolerant behavior.

The challenges one faces in society somehow relate to long-term personality changes and behavioral problems that may utterly harm the interests of the nation as a whole.

(3) Challenges of marital life:- Earlier this type of challenges were merged with the personal challenges but recently due to some major changes in the lifestyle of people and the rising expectations of youngsters regarding their life partners, marital challenges have been segregated as a separate type. People now have high expectations about their life partner. It is a tough job to find a compatible match for oneself and the next tougher task is to see that the marriage runs successfully. Nowadays marriages are broken due to small issues like ego clashes, misunderstandings, immaturity and strife on small issues. Hence it is an indispensable task that one should be fully prepared mentally to face the future challenges after marriage otherwise the marriage may be on rocks. Marriage as an institution is fast losing its sanctity as there are more divorces now and there is lack of patience, tolerance and maturity at some level. Today is the age of doing things fast without giving much thought to the issue. In case one finds a compatible life partner, then one should take care of all the things so that no tension develops in the married life. Understanding each other's nature, preferences, priorities, expectations and taking care of the comfort level of your partner are some basics which should be taken care of.

Marriage should not only be considered as an institution but as a commitment between two people towards a loving, affectionate, understanding and successful life ahead. If we go deep, marriage is a promise of two souls of not hurting each other, trusting each other even in the dire situations when no one else is trustworthy, taking care of the minutest necessities of your partner as a means of utmost care and hence we can say that marriage is a journey from a worldly companionship towards a divine relation of two souls when you seldom realize the fact that your life partner has changed into your soul mate. Just imagine how cruel it would be to bring such a beautiful relationship into jeopardy. Hence one should be careful while marrying but caring after marriage.

If you have entered into the world of marriage, then secure it by any means as it provides you with a person who is completely dedicated to you, who is all ears for you when the world has shut their ears for you, who lends you her/his shoulder when you need it the most, who understands the meaning of the warmth of your tears and who knows all the secrets behind your cold and warm smiles, who knows your needs and takes care of your desires and above all supports you at that point of age when even your children may go away from you. We will take a simple example as given below:-

Example (i):- Robert and Catherine knew each other for the past 2 years and then were planning to marry. After a period of long discussions and planning, they decided to marry. They tied the knot and were very happy. The happiness lasted for a year and a half and then started the problems. They started to fight at trivial issues and found no sense in spending time with each other as they have started losing interest in their wedded life. The repercussions of this were that Robert started spending more time outside with his friend circle and started avoiding Catherine, and she started feeling neglected and dejected. As Catherine used to remain at home, she had few friends and negative feelings with respect to their married life entered her mind. The prospects of their life were dismal but still there was one hope that they still loved each other. Both of them decided to introspect and evaluate the reasons behind their behaviors and found the major reason was that they knew each other's weaknesses and strengths very well before marriage and after some time of their marriage, both of them started feeling as though there was nothing interesting in the other.

Other reason was that although they cared for each other but didn't feel the need to express their love and care to the other partner in the absence of which the other one started feeling dejected and avoided. They worked upon their relationship that was in trouble and within months were counted among the happiest couples of the county. Hence, instead of thinking of breaking a marital relationship in problem, one must try to bandage it and wait for the healing of wounds which will lead to an everlasting, soulful and deeply beautiful relationship. So, guys, all the best for your future!

4. Emotional Challenges: - Such kinds of challenges are not explicit but implicit. Whenever a problem crops up, our attention is directed towards the apparent challenges but not the by-products of that problem which are emotional challenges. In case a person is facing marital challenges, it is but obvious that emotional challenges are attached with them as two people are in a deeply emotional relationship and hence even the trivialities hurt a lot.

So, in such cases, first of all emotional challenge should be dealt with and the other type later on as if a person is emotionally balanced, only then can he understand the whole scenario and further towards the solution of the problem. Similarly, the challenges of adolescent life are intertwined deeply with emotional challenges. As the young people easily get emotional when it comes to certain issues, hence, they should first be made to feel comfortable and then emotionally at ease. Similarly, challenges of love life are essentially concerned with the emotional life of people and it is also very tough to discriminate clearly between emotional challenges and love life challenges.

As there is no clear demarcation, the chances of a person getting confused between the two are more but however we can distinguish if some concepts are clear in our minds. In emotional challenges, one is concerned purely with emotions and they are easy to overcome and should be treated on priority basis but in love life challenges, the person is not only facing emotional disturbances but his view for life as a whole also gets vague and ultimately it becomes difficult to make such a person see the reality of the scenario.

A person if wishes can contribute towards the end of emotional problems in his life although it requires special and dedicated effort. Every person knows his weaknesses and the issues of his life over which he gets emotional, so the first thing one has to do is to segregate the issues on which he gets emotional as more sensitive and less sensitive areas.

One is harmed less by less sensitive areas and more by more sensitive areas as the former are common to most of the people and can be dealt with as they arise but the latter are much more person specific and if not dealt with in time can lead to bigger troubles. For becoming the troubleshooter of the more sensitive type of emotional issues, the first indispensable thing is that one should be honest with oneself and the second is that one should be harsh to oneself. After segregation of issues and coming to the major one, one should try to find out the reason behind getting so emotional over that issue again and again as it is usually of repetitive nature. We will go by the means of an example given below.

> **Example (i):-** Suppose a person X is in deep love with a person Y and both are unable to be together. The person X being very pragmatic is easily able to overcome this emotional encounter while on the other hand the person Y being very emotional and hypersensitive in nature is not being able to do so. First of all, Y thinks to take the help of a psychiatrist in overcoming this emotional problem, but then Y decides to be brave enough to face the situation itself. Y, here is a girl and she is brave enough. First of all she tries to find out the reasons behind not forgetting X. She finds out that X has some characteristics which she considers special and due to which she is not being able to forget him, i.e. X, her friend.
>
> Those qualities include his caring nature, adaptability, intelligence, and good personality. Then she introspects and finds that there are many other people with good personality in this world who impress her, many with intellect level higher than X

who are impressed by her, many people who would love to be adaptable, in case she gives them importance and her family and relatives are always with her to comfort her. She focused on all these things for sometime and found herself out of the emotional chaos.

This given example reveals the fact that our hearts are pure and innocent. An innocent heart can be deeply affected by so called love. I am using the term, "so called" as the true love is as rare as a pure pearl and what appears to be love to the youth of today is just fascination, attraction or obsession. When we get trapped in the web of this impure or illogical love, then the problems of various kinds emerge. Such challenges may relate to a person's psychology, his behavioral patterns, his attitudinal differences, his drooping confidence level, his ability to fight the life's other odds. If a person develops the will to overcome a problem, then the issue is half-resolved.

Example (ii):- In case, a person named Z loses a family member, then naturally the grief is deep. With passing time too, Z is unable to come to terms with his sorrow. He must understand a universal fact that this world is dynamic and ever-changing, hence nothing is permanent here. The deceased has just left his physical body in order to enter the astral body. Once Z accepts this law of nature, he will be able to overpower his grief.

Every human being whosoever comes on this earth makes several goals but the ultimate and supreme goal of mankind is to reach that Supreme power via the journey of life. One has to shed this worldly cloth of this physical body and wear the divine cloth of astral body and then blend with the Supreme Soul.

Thereafter starts the real journey, the journey of the soul, from the finite to the infinite, from the start of the knowledge to the assimilation of pure, spiritual and divine knowledge. The person Z cries because he feels the loss of love of the deceased person but he forgets that the deceased's soul has been in search of Godly love which now has been got by it. Z should think that no one has the right to stop someone from attaining the love of the

Almighty. Time of getting that love is different in various cases and nothing else. I and you, everyone will be blessed to go above, enter God's heart and get as much love as we can imagine. Z understood this hard fact and was happy for the soul of the dead thereafter.

5. Adaptability Challenges:- Every surrounding environment offers us different kinds of challenges but one challenge which is common to all, exists everywhere and spreads like a virus is adaptability challenge. As a virus is dormant outside but becomes alive on entering the body of the organism, similarly the adaptability challenge is not apparent from outside but it is our mind, heart and soul which confront with it, and overpowers it.

The family we live in consists of various members with different temperaments, values, expectations, priorities, and attitudes towards us. We face certain adaptability problems in the beginning years of our stay with the family but with the passing time, such issues get resolved. In certain extreme cases, an individual's continuous efforts to adapt to the family environment may fail, and he may not be able to find a comfortable cocoon for himself.

A school which is the most important part of a child's life after his family, is considered to be a safe, healthy and nourshing place for any child. School life looks very attractive and comfortable from outside but hidden ground reality is always awaiting the child. All the children have different qualities and vary from one another. Some are naughty, some docile, some laborious and some are nasty. Every child faces adaptability problems, only the degree varies depending upon the sensitivity level and attitude of children. As far as possible, one should try not to get perturbed by such factors and the parents should take special care their children in their formative years. This is the time period during which the overall development of a child takes place. The support system of the family, if strong can help the child face any situation. The children must be encouraged to share most of the tings with parents. It is not advisable to consult a doctor for such matters at the first instance. The medical practitioner will recommend medicines in most of the cases which will help the child outwardly but once if the child is severely hurt from inside and has taken has a thing to heart, the wound can become deeper with time. Such cases have become more prevalent nowadays and it later on may result into juvenile delinquency too.

Although such things are rare at college and university level, yet extreme cases of ragging in medical and engineering colleges crop up every year. By the time one enters into college or later into a university to pursue higher studies, the mind and the heart have become stronger so as to face the societal and environmental challenges.

When we talk of society, it's environment is getting worse day by day and there is no system to regulate emotional and psychological crimes like these. The biggest problem behind such issues is that if one kills a person altogether, he may be imprisoned for this heinous crime but if somebody totures a person on a regular basis and that too, indirectly, there is no clear punishment defined in the law of this nation. Such acts may deteriorate the mental stamina of the victim, can cause psychological stress and hypertension resulting in brain disorders like depression, Bipolar effective disorder and Schizophrenia. Today, in the society,everyone goes by his own wish without giving a thought to the fact that their action may wreck a life or kindle strife. All of us should try to make a change at our own level so that we may be able to make a big difference one day by collaborating with like-minded people.

Let's pledge that that as far as possible we will not become the disturbing element of the society. The below example will make the above described concept more clear:

Example (i):- M. K Narayanan is a famous writer, poet and novelist. He writes what he feels to be true from the bottom of his heart. This is theproblem with his writings is that they truly speak his mind and are not much market-oriented. As he writes on controversial issues, often people go against him and use vulgar language for him. After sometime, he became very perturbed and even took the decision of quitting writing forever. Then he consoled himself and came to understand the simple fact the people who were doing all this were not actually responsible for all this nonsense as they could not do anything else. Every individual has a knowledge sphere and everyone has a limit of curiosity and ability to learn. If some people were talking against him and were condemning his work, then it might be due to their limited knowledge sphere and limited capabilities to learn and grow. Those who do not want to learn & grow cannot be forced to do so but those who wanted to read his work, his poems, his novels, his prose writings, those who waited for his upcoming work should be the reason of smile, joy, motivation & living for him & not others.

Those who were doing this had that much knowledge only and could give which they were giving to him while he had a developed mind, farsightedness, and good vision which he was sharing with them. So, that was the end of the adaptability challenges in the life of M. K. Narayanan. Thereafter he was a happy man and created a number of useful works for the society that propelled the folks to think on contemptuous issues.

6. Professional Challenges: - Life is quite comfortable and soothing like fresh air until we live in the secure premises of our homes but as soon as we enter the outer world, the professional world clouds us and we come to face the pollution.

It is not a universal fact as there may be people who have very good experiences with their profession but generally the professional world of today lacks the air of pure and healthy competition. It is stuffed with the air of cut-throat competition, jealousies, ill-feelings, sycophancy and bad word of mouth. One should not feel oppressed by negative environment at work place as it affects the confidence level of yours and your career in the long run. Profession is something without which one cannot do. Everyone in the job world has to tolerate hostile atmosphere to some extent but that does not mean that one gets disappointed and lose hope. There are people who yearn for a good job and some even have to face the bleak prospects of getting a job at the first place, so in case you have got a job and there are some problems, you instead of quitting the job should think of finding a solution.

It is the testing time that teaches you how do deal with adversity, how to manage situations properly, and how to manipulate circumstances to your benefit to some extent. Workplace is the place where one comes to know about the worldly matters and the development of worldly wisdom takes place, otherwise at home one feels secure and comfortable.

If a person remains within the comfort zone, then there are less chances of him learning new & innovative things that have positive effect on his wisdom and growth. It is only when you sacrifice your comfort level that you learn many things in life and as it has been rightly said that knowledge has a price. So, in case you are a curious learner, an inquisitive mind, a searching soul, then be ready to sacrifice your comfort level. Beyond this, you will also learn to accept the hard realities of this materialistic world.

But nowadays several organizations are paying due attention towards good working environment and the development of healthy work culture as it will lead to fewer grievances from employees and better productivity. Grievance cells for employees have been established in almost all the organizations and various grievance handling procedures are being employed to reduce the complaints and to keep a check on the negative elements. So, in case you are facing tough situation at work, you can forward your concern through proper channel and wait for the results. If the problem still persists, then there are many alternate solutions available, one of which being change of job.

7. Challenges of Adolescent Life: - Adolescents are future makers of a nation and society. They are the ones who will decide the changes which will be made in lifestyle, behavior, attitude, perceptions, preferences, priorities and culture in future. They will become future leaders, teachers, doctors, engineers, lawyers, executives and will lead the nation towards progress. Adolescents should be taken proper care of as they are the roots and will grow into trees very soon. They are such flowers which by spreading the fragrance of brotherhood, respect, love, secularism, and freedom will unite every flower of the garden. They will become the torchbearers of democracy. Adolescent stage of a human being is very delicate. It should be dealt with proper

care and attention, else it may result into personal loss on one hand and societal devastation in the long-term.

During adolescent life, one has to face somewhat different kind of challenges. The person at this stage is neither a child nor an adult and gets confused over many issues. He feels like taking decisions of his life on his own but is interrupted by elders of the family who think him to be incapable of taking independent decisions. This is the stage when the mind of a person is about to reach the higher level of maturity and he starts making new perceptions regarding various things in life.

An adolescent person becomes a keen observer and is sensitive to the happenings of the surroundings. He starts understanding his responsibilities towards family, friends, society and the nation and becomes aware of his rights too. Most of the people fall in love during this phase of life and it is a matter of great concern as they may fall prey to wrong choice of the beloved, impatient decisions, emotional breakdowns and even suicidal attempts. Adolescents are like those sensitive flowers which need to be protected but at the same time require sunlight for blossoming.

As the mind and heart both are more susceptible to the negative thoughts and comments, hence, both the heart and the mind must be properly trained and managed by the self. One must also take the advice of elders, act with patience, develop a strong will power, use own intellect, do proper analysis of the whole scenario, and accept the truth. More than 90% of the problems during this period arise due to non-acceptance of truth. Some are unwilling to accept dejection from the other person or are unable to accept the reality of the scenarios; some are unwilling to accept the repercussions of a wrong decision taken by self; some unwilling to accept one's weaknesses; some unwilling to accept failure in studies; and some are unwilling to accept that have any problem. There are various kinds ofpeople but the question arises that how the acceptance of truth creates a difference in one's life.

The person who starts accepting the facts of his life and comes to terms with the reality of his life leads a peaceful life. I do not advocate the adjustment to the extreme level, but coming to terms with life's reality is different.Although it is not an easy task and requires honesty coupled with self and courage, yet if you do that, life becomes much easier for you. Till the time you run away from your own reality and continue finding faults with something or someone, you cannot mature. Anything outside you, any authority, person or situation cannot be held responsible for your present state of affairs. If this is a digestable fact for you, the complete dish of life is going to be tasty!

For inner self to grow and flower, you should feed it with self analysis, self awareness, and tons of honesty. Don't worry it is still less caloric than the high caloric and oily food you eat on a daily basis. This if taken into practice will fill your mind and heart with the necessary nutrients and will also take care of the fact that you don't get overweight by things like overconfidence. The person who knows himself better has more chances of early betterment. He will evaluate his strengths and weaknesses on a regular basis, will not be much perturbed by the outside world, will come to know the indispensables of his life, based on which he will decide his priorities in life. Above all, then he will chalk-out every plan of his life carefully keeping his caliber in mind, thus dimming the chances of failure in life ahead.

Hence, adolescent life is an important phase of one's life and should not be wasted.

8. Aging Challenges:- As soon as one enters old age, the world comes to a change. There are mainly three types of old people, one who are dejected by their families, second who have a wrong perception in their minds that people around them are neglecting them and they keep on harboring false notions in their minds and third type of people are those who are have an absolutely healthy thinking and feel good for everyone around. It is not the responsibility of their families only to look after them but the duty of the whole society towards them as they are the ones who have contributed a lot towards the development of society.

The people who are in their old years have contributed so many precious years of their life towards nation building, development of a strong foundation of the society and the giving of good values to the youngsters. We would never be able to know our culture, value-system and the contribution of freedom fighters in the freedom struggle if our grand parents were not there.

Those who have the blessings of elders are the luckiest people in the world. There are people who understand the concept of generation gap and accept the fact that youngsters nowadays like to spend more time with their peer group. By having such thinking, they never feel avoided or neglected. Still every one of us tries to spend as much time as possible with the elders and believe me you will feel cared for. We think that we care for them but as it is a two-way process, we are also cared for.

By just investing some of our time, we gain so much in return like abundant love, endless care, valuable advice, nurturing feeling and the warmth of an emotional bond. Old people can be termed as altruists also as they are almost in the end phase of their lives and will always give selfless love. Such people are like the banyan tree which is very old but still gives shadow to others and every passenger who wants to take rest can have a wink of good sleep under it. As "Old is Gold", is a famous saying, so all the old people are precious for all of us.

9. Fitness Challenges:- We live in an unhealthy environment and thus it becomes all the more important to take care of our health. Health is a very broad term. It is a combination of physical health, mental health, emotional health, spiritual health and creative health. I agree to the fact that in earlier times, the term health was restricted to physical health only but after intensive research of long time, dedicated efforts of doctors, scientists, nutritionists, spiritual teachers, psychologists, and other health specialists, a conclusion has been drawn that the term health cannot be narrowed down to physical health only. Hence, precisely the above definition of health was figured out. To stay completely healthy, we should take utmost care of all the aspects. Good health is a 360 degree phenomenon.

Physical health implies taking care of our body as a whole including all the organs and organ-systems. Everyone individual is very busy nowadays and the corporate culture is increasing day by day. Due to this enhanced corporate culture and the fast paced lifestyle, the culture of junk food is becoming a major problem nowadays. This issue has given rise to obesity and other related disorders. We should discipline our lives and curb the habit of eating fast food and this is one of the ways we can get rid of this trouble to much extent. The other ways being, inculcating the habbit of practicing yoga and pranayama daily, walking daily to the extent one can, doing the household chores oneself physically instead of doing them mechanically altogether or by engaging helping hands of someone else. These ways are not magic wands, one has to go a long way even after starting on this path!

What according to a lay man is the definition of a sound mind? A person with a sound mind can be described as the one who humbly leads his life without raising his or her voice against anything wrong happening in the society or surroundings. He may also be the person who has double standards of life, one for his family and the other for the society, or he may be the one who is afraid to help someone in need just because he is afraid of any kind of loss. A person who does not listen to his heart and wishes and simply leads the life of a coward throughout may also be deemed as a person with a sound mind. Definitely, all the individuals who are not taking pills for any mental disorder are supposed to have sound minds.

It means anybody who is clinically not suffering from any kind of brain disorder is supposed to have a sound mind. Yes, definitely if you are one of the above, you are lucky in a way. But, my dear, as per science, not even a single individual in this universe can be stated as hundred percent sane.

We all have various mental capabilities and we act accordingly. Our behavior in different situation of life depends on our collection of experiences, our apprehensions and to much extent what circumstances we face repeatedly. Suppose a person never faces the struggle of an examination, he will never come to know the strategies adopted to clear the examination. In the same manner, those who face the adversity of mental challenges better know, than an otherwise normal person to confront such type of challenges. Later such challenges may become like the season of autumn in that person's life, which comes and then after sometime is replaced by the spring of love and care.

The problem that exists in our society is that diseases related to our brain have a stigma attached to them due to which many people in our nation still don't get them treated as they feel ashamed of the disease. There is no reason to feel so as just like diabetes mellitus, coronary heart diseases or high blood pressure, it is a problem related to our brain, which is also an important organ of human body. Some people are afraid of the society, and, in case they get themselves treated, they hide this fact from others. But very few people are aware of the fact that a huge number of people in this world suffer from such disorders; the only difference may be in the type or degree. The society should be empathetic towards such people instead of being sympathetic as sympathy generates a sense of pity and empathy generates a feeling of care and belongingness. Together, we can resolve this matter!

Emotional health is an important aspect of the wider concept of health as an emotionally unhealthy person cannot rise much in life and due to clouded vision, is not able to see the things clearly. First, we should treat ourselves on the emotional front and then should work upon future plans.

Spiritual health is also very essential as it is only when we reach the sphere of spirituality, that we experience tranquility, peace and discover harmony with ourselves. A spiritual person is not a liability on society but he becomes as asset. He is the one who spreads peace everywhere and is ready to help mankind anytime. As we come in touch with spirituality, our concepts of life become clear and we are above the clouds of vagueness, unclarity and ignorance. We come to know that this world is one reality but the ultimate reality is that we have come from the divine and we have to reach the divine. Everything we collect, every relation we cherish, every desire we have will be left here, every chord with this world will be broken one day and we will go to merge into the divine.

Creative health is another form of health which is necessary for the complete development of an individual. If one involves oneself in creative pursuits, then the journey of life becomes much interesting and easier. Creativity is embedded in every person to some extent; the need is only to give a proper direction to it. The person, who channelises his positive and negative energies towards creative pursuits, wins the race of life at the end. In case the creativity in a person finds no way out, it can have negative ramifications on that person's overall development. Creativity also leads to the divine as one who is creative feels much closer to God. Creative health serves as a nutrient for good mental health too. The more you engage yourself in creativity, the more tranquility your mind experiences. Thus every wise person either engages himself in creative things or take keen interest in creative works of others.

10. Challenges of Love Life:- Every soul falls in love. Some fall in love with the member of opposite sex, some fall in love with a friend, some love their parents, brothers or sisters dearly and some fall in love with a famous personality who may be a social figure. We will be dealing with the type of love youngsters fall in. Some mature and blossomed souls fall in love with their nation too!

Mostly teenagers and people in their twenties fall in love with the member of opposite sex. Sometimes they are attracted towards a person and falsely take it as love. The other things which are mistaken as love include crush, fascination and emotional dependency. Such kind of love may prove fatal for that specific person who is at fault. It is one sided love and when the illusion is over, the one who is serious, enters into problem.

As this is that age group in which a person is highly sentimental and emotional over such issues, the person should take care of some aspects. He should know how to demarcate properly between attraction and true love, should try to build a healthy relationship and not a relation based on hasty decisions and sentiments and should be strong enough to face dejection from the other person.

Love challenges break the will power of a person, weaken his confidence, cloud his vision and clarity towards sensitive matters. After failure in love, an individual starts underestimating himself. The hazards of love life, shattered dreams and broken heart can be long-lasting.

When it comes to emotions, especially the emotion of love, the question who is more emotional , a girl or a boy does not arise. All have equal tendencies of falling in love, crying after heart breaks, valuing the smallest gifts of the boyfriend or the girlfriend, listening to romantic songs or ghazals for longer duration, working absent mindedly, and so on. The list is long enough.

Love is to be nurtured carefully after finding the correct partner at the right age and time. People say, "falling in love", but I believe in " rising in love". A person can learn a lot after coming in contact with the other. There are lot more positive attributes which are still hidden from us. We have to grasp them.

A girl may take time to forget her love but once a boy loves someone truly, he will never forget his love. If you truly love a person, then you will think of his/her growth. If love is true, one doesn't fall in love but both the persons rise in life, move ahead, and pray for each other's overall growth and development. One should be wise enough to understand the fact that in case you are not able to get lifelong companionship of your lover, then it should not be a matter of sorrow and one should always pray for the well-being of one's partner.

Love is basically of three types including selfish love, symbiotic love and divine love. Selfish love is that kind of love in which one person or both the persons love each other for their selfish interests. Such interests include the need of being loved, cared for, the desire of being heard and so on.

Such kind of love may give immediate gratification of some kind but is lethal in the long run. Symbiotic love is that type which is normally found in this society. In it, the two people love each other deeply,are benefitted by each other but have the concern for their own desires too. They fulfill each other's emotional needs and also long for the lifelong companionship. As both of them are benefitted, it is regarded as symbiotic kind of love.

The third and the purest kind of love is divine love. Divine word not only relates to the Almighty, but being divine means being in your natural self all the time. If you are a base person and has not upgraded your inner self yet, be like that. Do not try to become or show what you are not. If are internally uplifted, reveal your shine and wisdom to others so that they can benefit. All the beings must strive towards the achievement of divinity but none should take a wrong path.

In divine love, we feel as if it is all over yet we are breathing and then we are being told the value and meaning of our present breaths by the Supreme Soul. Somebody who is divine is pure in his thoughts, and deeds. There are not many layers left.The person does not expect anything in return for his love and is always ready to make sacrifices for thy beloved. Such kind of love is rarely found and is the most giving kind of love. When we fall in love with God, it is also termed as divine love. Love is dear to God, so those who love someone truly always get the blessings of God.

We have discussed ten challenges of life and to some extent the methods to face those challenges. Challenges are a part and parcel of life but we should face them courageously and should have a proper attitude towards life. Howsoever tough a challenge is, if we apply the right proportion of the mixture of strength, emotional balance, correct decisions, strong will power and right use of intellect, then that challenge can be overcome. I have deciphered my thoughts in the beginning of the chapter in few lines too.

Although facing challenges is a tough task;
Yet during this task, we have many questions to ask;
To ourselves and find out their answers;
This creates harmony and makes many things clear;
We come to know of our shortcomings;
Strive for perfection and increase strengths;
There is a bunch of many more things to do;
We don't falter again and there is nothing to redo;
Facing challenges makes us strong;
We discover our potential and lessen chances to be wrong!

Chapter - 4

Facing Challenges of Life

Big or small, every moment is a challenge. There are challenges that are very obvious and there are some which are not that obvious. There are some challenges that are real and there are some which are illusionary. We can deal with some quite easily while on the other hand we should be well equipped to deal with the remaining. There is not a single doubt in that one should have strong will power and determination to deal with any kind of challenge. Two other assistants which help in dealing with challenges are a peaceful mind and focused attitude. Combining all these and with the help of Almighty, one can face and deal even with fierce challenges of life.

In case one feels weak and has lack of strong will, one can borrow it and there is nothing wrong in doing it. There are situations when one is faced with a tough challenge and is simultaneously devoid of full strength, then one can either take inspiration from an external source directly or indirectly which is both reliable and accessible.

The prominent question arising in your minds must be that can one really borrow or develop strong will power and strength in the hour of need. The answer to this question is in the affirmative. Strong will power is our input or the fuel which is burnt at times when we have to face challenges. The direct sources from which one can borrow inner strength and will power can be an understanding person who is near to you and reliable and can be a family member, friend, colleague, a well wisher, or a consultant. Such people can directly help us in difficult and strenuous situations and come in the category of direct sources.

Other category is difficult to accept as our minds are fed with this myth that anybody away from us can't inspire us to this extent that we gain something worthwhile from them. Indirect sources of inspiration include people whom we idolize in our lives. In tough times, we can always remember their examples and tell our hearts and analyze in our minds that if those people in spite of facing such big challenges have reached to their respective positions in life, then why can't we face the challenges of our lives courageously and reach our aim? The other indirect and the biggest source of motivation for all of us in all odd situations is the love of Almighty which is always there for us. He is the torchbearer of the lives of all human beings, he spreads the fragrance of love for us and we can always feel His love whenever we feel like feeling it. In case one is trapped in any tricky situation, or is facing the toughest challenge of life, just close your eyes think of Him and ask Him for the required strength and He will definitely bless you. Rather, there is a discrepancy here that whether this is an indirect source or the most direct source of motivation, inspiration and strength, we have. If we are able to set up a direct contact with Him by our true devotion and dedication, we will not need any other help or guidance.

By all these sources, at first it appears that we are borrowing will power for sometime only and we are not confident of ourselves but in the long run we find that it help develop our own will power and enhances our strength. All these efforts motivate us permanently unless and until one is completely shattered.

Such people should have faith in God as He is the ultimate source of strength. For such extreme cases, it is advisable that with undeterred faith in God, they should try to seek motivation until they achieve their aim and overcome the challenge. This path will provide such people with two other things that are worth getting, peace of mind and inner satisfaction. So while trying to get out of a situation temporarily, one develops a strong will, inner strength and also a strong decisive power. Hence, we come to the conclusion that there is no harm in getting help from outside when in need and rather it is beneficial for us as it serves dual purposes.

There is another aspect which should be kept in mind is that there are different kinds of challenges and all of them require separate techniques to be solved. As we have already discussed that there are ten types of challenges that exist, all of them require some special treatment. As such there is no concrete way of facing a specific challenge, one should think, analyze and then decide that according to the situation what can be done?

Challenges are sometimes situation and person specific, so it depends on person to person and the specific situation that how a challenge will be dealt with. One thing that surely helps a person in distress is that one should never lose hope. Hope takes the cart of your life out of the mud of adversity and drives it forward towards the destination.

Chapter - 5

Materialism

Materialism is usually considered as the urge to gain worldly wealth and attachment to materialistic things of the world. Materialistic things consist of money, power, name, fame, a big house to live in, a car with a chauffer, your children studying in big convent school and the list goes on and on.

People who usually say that materialism is bad are the ones who themselves believe in it but may have failed in life to gain materialistic wealth or feel jealous for others who have gained much heights in life. I strongly believe in the fact that materialism has several positive aspects and is not at all a bad thing.

But the only thing that should be taken care of is that the race for wealth should have some limit, as, if it is endless, it can create problems too. "Excess of anything is bad", is rightly said. So, one should be cautious that he should not be in the race of gaining unlimited wealth, extraordinary status in the society, immeasurable success and things like that.

The positive aspects of materialism are also many. It inculcates the feeling of competition, a thrust for success, provides motivation for achieving something worthwhile in life and drives one towards higher horizons in life. If the back force of materialistic attitude is not there, success is not much assured. It is one of the driving forces behind gaining wealth and success leaving other factors like earning for livelihood, for the well being of the family and self satisfaction of being worthwhile.

Not everything that is not purely divine is bad. Even God favors a person who fulfills all the worldly duties and still is true to his conscience. Those who want to tread the path of spirituality are surely less inclined towards materialism but they too have to pay attention towards their basic duties and responsibilities. Moreover, there is no clear demarcation between things that are linked to materialism and those which are not linked to it.

Moreover, materialism is nothing more than yearning for materialistic pursuits or possessing the desire to own some of the best materialistic possessions of the world. If we have a deep look at it, it is not at all a negative thing. God has created man with some basic qualities, one of which is the spirit to live a better life and to provide the loved ones, all the amenities of life. How can an intention to move towards betterment in life and to succeed in life, wrong? It is only some people's perception that everyone who is materialistic is selfish and nothing else. There are some other misconceptions related to this concept too. Everyone who is born in this world is selfish and persons reach to the height of selflessness are rare.

So, if anyone comes to me and says that he is doing something selflessly, the thing is indigestible to me. The Supreme Soul Himself teaches us to take care of ourselves as He has made us well-equipped for facing any situation in life and striving for a better and comfortable life. The only thing that we have to keep in mind is that we should do something for our fellow human beings too and should not indulge in excess of anything. If we desire for something, then it should not turn into an obsession and should have clearly defined limits.

Some people even call you materialistic in order to discourage you or to make you guilty conscious as their intention is to stop or reduce your growth. I call such elements of the society as growth hampering viruses. Their number may vary according to the environment and the amount of your success. The wealthier a person becomes, the more such viruses surround him.

Hence one should possess a well developed and well regulated self-analysis system which helps to provide a regular check on behavior, growth patterns, thinking and changing tendencies. Such a system avoids over indulgence in any kind of materialistic pursuit, and it also diminishes the chances of slavery of any vice. Thus to conclude we should not favor extremity of materialism but should not avoid it altogether. We may strive for materialistic pursuits of any kind but our soul should not be a slave of such longings.

Growth in any way is a human being's right and we cannot deny anyone this right and we are no one to formulate laws for others when we ourselves lack in many aspects. Degree may vary but every one of us wants a comfortable life and fulfilling relationships.

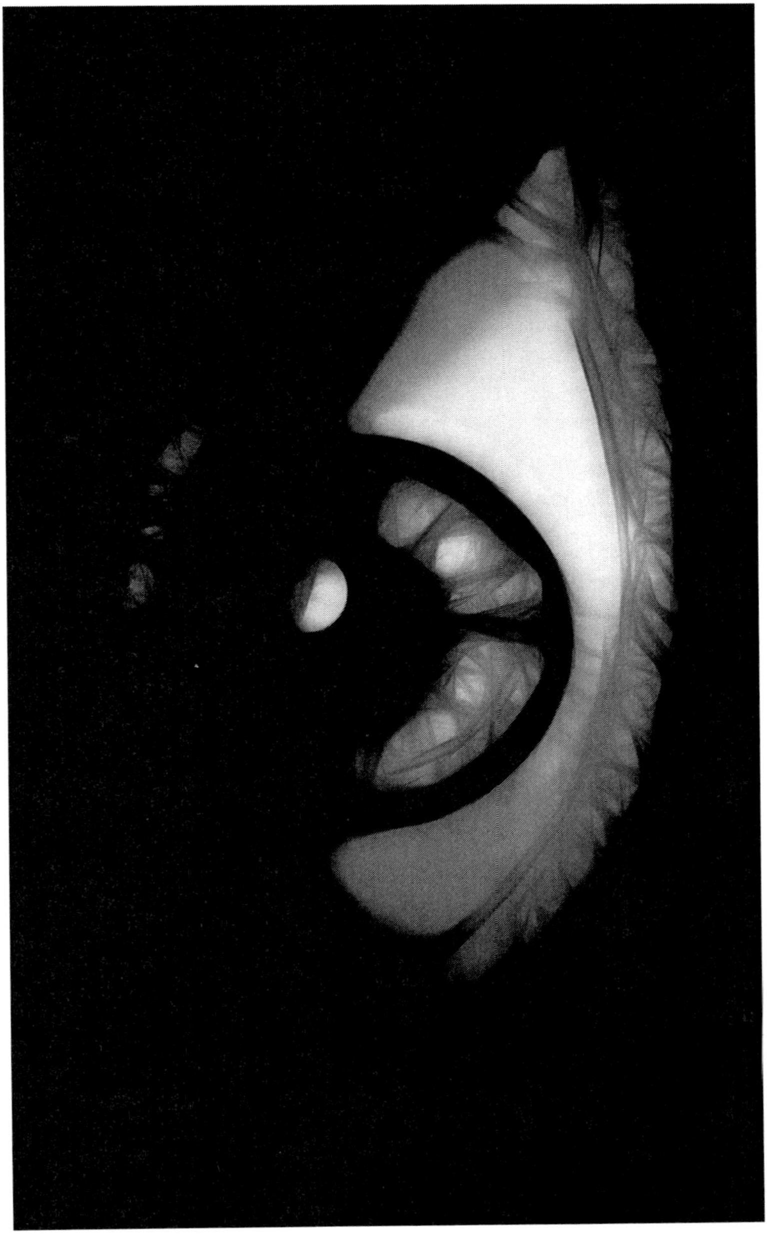

Spirituality and religion are born twins;
They are linked closely with the same strings;
If one is not sought for, you cannot get the other;
But one who is serious need not bother;
Both of them form the two strands of Divine Genome;
Similar in nature, they belong to the same form.

Chapter - 6

Spirituality & Religion

Spirituality and religion are such nicely intertwined with each other that it is a tough job to see them separately. They are just like the two strands of Human DNA that form the backbone of human genome. Likewise, spirituality and religion both form the backbone of human life. Without both of them, we would not be able to stand straight in our lives and will feel morally bankrupt in a sense.

Both stand like pillars for us throughout our lives, guiding us through the darkness of selfishness, morally uprooted environment, ignorance, myths, downgrading of human values and takes us towards the divine light of compassion among human beings, affection for all the creatures, knowledge, high morals and values, devotion for God and a clear conscience. These things too have a value which one has to pay that is true devotion for the Supreme Soul, adoption of the principles of humanity, praying for the betterment of others, and working for universal peace and compassion for all the creatures on earth.

There is no other heaven on earth or elsewhere except that we being humans, behave in a human way towards all the creatures, love all, harbor no ill feelings in our hearts, lead a peaceful and spiritual life following our respective religious principles and give equal respect to all other religions and faiths as we respect our own religion. God does get delighted when we remember Him but He gets more delighted when we remember our duties towards our fellow human beings and hurt nobody. He doesn't keep any account of our good and bad doings but He does read faces and comes to know whether we have hurt a soul or not, He does come to know about our feelings for others when we face Him.

Religion is the guide and spirituality is the path that we have to tread in order to reach the Divine Light. Religion provides all the prerequisites and the guiding principles for following the path of spirituality and the path of spirituality acts as the torchbearer for the followers who are sincerely devoted to the Supreme Soul. Both of these are indispensable for spiritual and divine success. It is the real success of life, all others are just illusionary. When a person is inclined towards spirituality, he moves towards the spheres of tranquility, harmony, devotion and divine wisdom. Religion behaves like a father and guides one to the path of righteousness, justice, brotherhood, unity and peace. It is religion that teaches us the value of humanity and describes the principles of humanity in a crystal clear way. Religion does not let us divert from the right way of living. By the means of preachings of different incarnations of God, religion shows the right way of living. It also proves that even God in His various incarnations during different periods has followed the principles of justice, humanity and equality and fulfilled all His worldly duties and responsibilities. Hence we are taught that everyone who takes birth in this world has to abide by the worldly rules and should not abandon his duties and will have to pay the price of wrong doings. Talk about religion cannot finish in few words as it is vast sea of knowledge whose one shore is related to this world and the other shore is related to the divine. One starts from this world and after gaining and implementing the given knowledge reaches the divine, and thus a life is regarded a true success when on reaching the other shore we become one with the Almighty.

But if you think of the path that you have to follow, you have to look towards spirituality. If religion is the father that tells us the entire procedure one has to follow in order to reach the divine, then spirituality is the mother that tells us exactly how to follow that procedure in a very tender manner. Spirituality in real sense is the path one has to follow to find the divine light. It is not very easy but a true devotee who is fully determined and wants to unfold the mystery of life to reach the Divine can reach his goal. One has to forget the world and live in the present moment and while enjoying those precious moments, the connection with the Divine can be set up. When one reaches that stage, there is no "I "and everything unites into one and form the whole. Once you unite into the whole, the tears dry up, the troubles vanish, the grievances end, the selfishness perishes, and we feel the ultimate divine peace. Then God embraces us and our journey of life ends and we move beyond that into the world of the Divine. Hence, it is spirituality that becomes the path, treading which we get this supreme joy.

Although, people take religion and spirituality as one, we have discovered minute differences between them. The person who knows these find it easy to follow both. Though these differences exist between the two, both lead to the Supreme Soul who is the Creator of this whole world and others too if they exist. So one who wants to gather the knowledge of any of these aspects, he must dip himself a little bit into the divine waters of the other. Both go hand in hand like fast friends and have the resemblance of twins as both are eternal. Hence one should always welcome the knowledge of religion with open hands as it often guides us to the path of purity, righteousness and humanity. And one should be able to raise oneself to the level from where the destination of spirituality becomes crystal clear as it embraces a human being and lands us in a literally different world of tranquility, and happiness and satisfaction is also rendered to us once we step up into the realm of spirituality.

awareness
acceptance
affection
compassion
trust
faith
gratitude
appreciation
understanding
respect
equanimity
attention
wisdom
curiosity
patience
confidence
inclusion
calmness
clarity
creativity
courage
non-judgment
presence
Desire
Wanting
Impression
Inclination
Strategy
Identification
Pleasure
Discomfort
Habit
Linkage
Contrast
Likeness
Meaning
Judgment
Knowledge
Arousal
Pain
Experience
Imitation
Custom
Self-image
Reflexes
Aversion
Role
Memory
Belief
Familiarity
Insecurity
Perspective
Adaptation
Difference
Reaction
Comfort
Similarity
Tradition
Narrative
Expectation
Resource
Demeanor

When one knows the Self;
It gives us the necessary help.
To meet the Supreme Being;
And it is the purest thing
When we find the divine;
Our soul and heart shine!

Chapter - 7

The Self

Which is the undiscovered abode in our lives? Do you want to connect with it? Do you want to know who are you? Do you want to unfold the mystery of your life? Then you may be helped after reading this.

How many of us are well acquainted with the self? Once we know the self, the obvious and prominent problems find solutions for themselves. We become aware of the inner self, the self that is shadowed with materialism of this world but the self that is the picture of the divine. We mostly boast of knowing others and the world but what a pity! We are not familiar with our own selves.

Knowing oneself is the first step of the ladder that takes us to the Supreme Being and allows merging completely with Him. We are talking of the puzzles of life and as we move ahead on the path of self-knowledge, self-analysis and introspection, the hidden fact comes forth and we feel the bliss of tranquility. The way we nurture our aims, ambitions, desires and values in life, the same way we have to nourish our inner self.

We cannot abandon ourselves and lookout for our desired answers elsewhere. God created us and he also created the solutions to all our problems and queries within us. Hence, all the required solutions are embedded in our inner self or the conscience. The thin line that we have to cross to reach there lies between searching the solution and knowing the problem.

When we stop searching for the solution and transgress our thoughts towards knowing the problem, all the misery comes to an end. We no more regret, fret and mourn. From this worldly abode, we reach the undiscovered abode, the abode where the divine lies and the self. And then, we just enjoy, feel, and celebrate the divine bliss. We stop consuming the poison of unnecessary fears, hyped expectations, and shallow attitudes and thinking. Rather, we assimilate the snowy divinity and have a sip of a mixed juice of tranquility, harmony, and peace. We come to know of the transformation going on within us and start having a feel of the newly wedded relation between us and the Supreme Soul.

Thereafter, starts a new journey, a journey where both the partners move ahead towards a new destination, following a virgin path, hand in hand. The partners are we and the Supreme Being, the destination is peace and purity and the path that is always person specific and is new for every follower, is the undiscovered abode. This undiscovered abode is the knowledge of the self as after knowing it, more than half the battle is won. The tuning and cooperation between both the treaders of the path is must. As every successful completion of a mission requires good understanding and chemistry on the part of both the partners, this coverage of this different path requires excellent chemistry between us and the Almighty. We should become firm devotees of Him and He should care of us which is but obvious.

Now, the question that pops up in our minds is that, do the divine lives with the self? Yes, the answer is in the affirmative. God didn't divide Himself and us. It is our knowledge and assumption that is biased and wrong. As our self comes from the divine and the divine rests in the self, there lies an unbreakable string between the both. Rather, it would be appropriate to mention here that the pure inner self is not separate from the divine. The way of knowing the self is very easy for those who have the pure desire to do so.

The term, "getting the self", used by some people is not considered appropriate by me, the reason being, self can only be known, never achieved like any other materialistic pursuit. The path that one has to tread to find the inner self and knowing it thoroughly is person specific. It is not like yoga, meditation, or any other kind of karma-kanda that has to be performed in a prescribed manner.

If a person doesn't believe in any kind of method but firmly believes in God, then his way to the divine also goes through finding the mystery of the self. If we don't know the basics, how can we be aware of the advanced facts?

In a similar fashion, if we don't unfold the self created by the Supreme Being, how can we reach the mysterious facts of the Almighty's kingdom? We have to take the initiative and only then we will be helped by Him at every step. Prior taking any decision, one should keep in mind this very fact that as nearer you come to your self, farther you go from other people near you. This is a hard reality, recognized by few. Some people acknowledge this at the beginning while others come to know of this fact later on. But the positive aspect is as you have started becoming a better human being in your search for the self, your worldly relations are not spoiled. Rather, you become more considerate, compassionate, patient, tolerant and loving. People start loving you more than ever before. It is like you come to know of the reality; still you follow all your duties. And the same thing can be learnt by the teachings of the Gita where it has been clearly mentioned that one should do one's duties faithfully without considering the outcome. It also teaches us that even if we are aware of all the realities, we shouldn't be dragged away from our path to righteousness.

Knowing the self is not a destination, it is an ongoing journey which brings pleasures and sorrows, successes and failures, sense of achievement and feeling of loss in packets of equal quantities. One has to be a true devotee of the Supreme Being, determined to tread this adventurous path, willing to sacrifice some of the precious things to keep on going on this path, and should be open-minded to welcome the surprises of life with joy and warmth.

Universe has a very stern rule for those who want to get anything and it is that the seeker should be a go-getter, a person with 'never say die' attitude, and not a guy who loses heart at trivial issues. He should be able to take success and failure at same length and must be broad minded enough to understand both the implicit and explicit meanings of the ways of nature to make him understand the various things. In a similar manner, if you want to know the self, you are a seeker and hence should possess all the qualities of a good seeker. It is obviously not a child's play but those whose heart and soul is as clear and innocent as a child get it faster. The concept of the self is very deep, the more deep one dives into these waters, the deeper the ocean grows. There is a virtual reality or existence of every individual which is apparent to all. There exists another hidden self of all which sometimes the person is unable to recognize. When one reaches that zone of self-realization, the distance is not far of to the destination of unwind the self totally. Every person's personality has layers and the deepest layer can be termed as the self. It is usually that part of the Zohari Window, which we don't know and the others also are unaware of.

The attempts to demarcate the power of the Almighty and the power of an individual self will go in vain. The two powers are one and the same. When we are faced with tough terrains, we call the power of the Almighty within and suddenly we are reenergized, full of motivation, confidence, will power and focus. All this is done by focusing on the innermost levels of our soul. It provides us with all that required spirit and power. Hence, the God also wants that we being humans must explore the unlimited potential and power within and perform nicely for the betterment of all the living beings including the flora and the fauna!

Once we come to know of the Self and come at terms with it and are in good harmony with it, come nearer to the Divine too.

Sky is the limit for those who dare;
For those who take proper care;
And have in them, the spirit and fire;
Find the path to the thing they desire;
They own the strong will and don't hire;
Life takes them to places higher and higher!

Chapter - 8

The Inner Zeal

Wake up! Have you met a friend within you? Or have you ever realized that the real motivator is just inside you? Did you ever try to find the solutions to the trickiest and the hardest of your problems with the help of your own self? The answer to all these questions lies here, just in this chapter.

People! Very often we land ourselves in tricky, strugglesome, and time consuming situations where we are unable to find solutions to small and big troubles of our daily lives. We find ourselves in such pathetic situations where we have the solutions but they don't fit in the sockets of our problems. Here starts the real problem, the problem of getting demotivated, discouraged and depressed. Life nowadays is not that easy as it used to be in yesteryears as now we have big hopes, big dreams, unalterable situations, weaker bonds, complex relationships, vacuumated hearts, and weaker will powers.

Everything can be possible if we start correcting ourselves and the sphere around us to much extent. To start with, first of all we should start practicing meditation and yoga. Sounds very obsolete, right! But these are the two things if incorporated in our lives can do wonders for us and help us in developing a strong will power. Efforts have to be put to achieve everything and they may vary in degrees. Having a rock-like will is a boon for anyone in this universe. Without a strong will, we may wither but not flower.

Our mind is like a little bud and it needs to be given free space to flower and spread its fragrance for our prosperity. In this small bud, there lies a huge treasure already and when we try to find solutions of various issues from it, we get the appropriate solutions. A strong will power acts like sunshine for the growth of our brain and hence helps us. As, when faced with the dire circumstances of this life, we need experience and wisdom combined, the brain should be well equipped with a strong will and wisdom and clarity. So, give space to your brain to grow, respire and flower.

We guys have started caring less for human relationships, bonding of the hearts and more for the longevity of the relationships and the long lasting effects of relationships on our lives. Don't you think it is a narrow and mechanical thinking? It has less touch of love, passion and care and more of hidden selfish motives. In a relationship, it is not important that two people will be together tomorrow or not but what matters is the depth, the purity of feelings. These things are as important as the development of a strong will power in a person. If you have emotional security, it provides you with the required strength to deal with adversity. Complex relationships and weaker bonds cloud the mind of a person, therefore resulting in the failure to deal with life's challenges.

All the above mentioned things constitute the inner zeal. That zeal takes you forward in life. The same zeal helps you in finding solutions to most of your problems in life. You want to do something and you are unable to pursue it, is a common scenario. So, you should consider all the major factors and prepare yourself well for it and then go ahead to achieve!

The last but not the least thing that should be taken care of is that we should never loose our ties with reality. One should be optimistic but realistic too. We should not think of conquering the world in a short span or time or changing ourselves altogether within few weeks. Every task has approximate time limit attached to it within which it can be achieved. Likewise, there are some requirements for every achievement which must be met to achieve it. If we correctly assess our potential, set our goals right, and with proper planning and time management move forward, destination will be right there.

It doesn't matter how long you go;
It doesn't matter how high you reach;
It is not a matter of theory and preaches;
It is not a matter of trivial clichés;
What matters after all is your Attitude;
That decides your Spiritual Altitude!

Chapter - 9

Spiritual Altitude

In the previous chapters, we have discussed the self and the inner zeal. If we have a close look at the two, both are related to each other, one being the destination and the other being one of the ways to reach there. If we have the inner zeal in us and our aim is to know the self, then the path is not uneven for us as one of the major requirements is met.

Moreover, after knowing the self, reaching the Divine is truly easier. Spirituality is definitely not only linked to the Divine, rather it is concerned with the whole of the Divine, i.e. divinity. All creatures, the whole universe, the whole of humanity, and the whole of the Divine are included in spirituality. Divine and the universe created by it are inseparable.

One who denounces humanity and the whole creation of the Divine, if boasts of practicing and preaching spirituality, makes me laugh. One who doesn't understand the basics of nature's laws and humanity is never able to reach the depths of spirituality. So, one who knows the Self also embraces the wholeness of the Supreme Being. Half of the path of spirituality is covered once you get to know the self and the later is covered by developing an inner zeal, motivation, the right attitude towards life and living, and determination to overcome all the challenges and obstacles that may come in between you and the destination.

By spiritual altitude, we not only mean the spiritual heights reached by a person but also the way, the means that are deployed to attain those heights. Likewise, in our lives, what matters at the end is the inner satisfaction derived from not our successes or failures but the means deployed by us to achieve those desired heights in our lives. Only our conscience knows it better than anyone else in this world that how satisfied we are from our successes or how sad we are at our failures. We may reach immeasurable heights and still find at the core of our hearts, the seeds of dissatisfaction or we may be utter failures in the opinion of the world and may enjoy the bliss of happiness somewhere in our lives. Thus, we may come to a perpetual conclusion that be it happiness or joy, be it melancholy or sorrow, all are least attached to the successes and failures of our lives and vice-versa.

If we have an in-depth look at the name spiritual altitude, we may ourselves feel that this is less related to the heights of spirituality rather more related to the depth of spirituality. In case we want to reach the heights of a thing, we need to equip ourselves with the tools of focused determination, persistent hard work, undeterred willpower, strong heart and good motives and moles in general. But, if we want to reach the depth of something, we must develop in ourselves, the poignant qualities of godly goodness, pristine purity, the will to embody the whole of the thing, and the deadly determination to get the maximum knowledge.

I hope I am not confusing you guys. By knowledge, I mean here that the knowledge of the basics of life especially the knowledge of the Self. Do not be mistaken and mingle it with the knowledge of the Divine as we can never know the Divine, we can only love Him, accept Him, offer prayers to Him and can identify ourselves with Him. Those who would just like to gather knowledge of spirituality or the Divine lands in futility and all their efforts go in vain. The reason behind this is the nature of the Divine which is felt and got by the persons who love Him and not those who try to know Him. Once you decide to know something, we stop loving it and all our efforts go waste in just getting something which is as unimportant as a little knowledge. Whereas the fact is that when we are passionate about one thing, we get it without gathering much knowledge, especially in the case of the Supreme Power.

When one decides to climb the ladder of spirituality, one should devoutly worship the Almighty. One must try to become one with God and no space should be left between the two. If we want to talk about the measures of attaining this aim in the path of spirituality, then I must say the best method is detachment. Detachment should be there not only from materialistic pursuits but also from any spiritual aim, divine desire or any other kind of ambition. Materialistic pursuits are said to be and known as the biggest hindrances in the way of the respective destination. One should detach oneself from every kind of attachment and not only from the materialistic aims and desires, is a fact known to the few.

I hope I have made myself pretty clear and the rest would be done in the later part of this chapter too. Detachment of what kind is needed will become clear from the given example.

For e.g. (1):- James and Sierra were two people who wanted to attain spiritual heights. Both were determined to climb the ladder of spirituality with some basic differences among them. James on the one hand was impulsive, and always in a hurry kind of person. He wanted to achieve his aim as soon as possible. Whereas Sierra on the other side was a composed girl who devoutly worshipped the Divine but she too wanted to reach some spiritual heights in her lifetime. The latter being the common thing among both, both were unable to understand that despite being so devout followers of religion, and such true worshippers why are they unable to get their goals. One cloudy day, both were moving on a lonely road and it started raining. Then an old passerby who was going on the same way commented that, "unless you people become like this rain, you will not be able to achieve your aim". Thorough thinking of the whole night landed them nowhere.

Then, both of them searched for the place where the man lived and asked him the meaning of his saying. Then the person told them that both of them were clinging strongly to their thoughts of attaining something, and that thought in them is restricting them from achieving their divine goals. Unless and until one is detached from everything and thought, one is never able to reach any heights. Thereafter, Sierra left every worldly pursuit and also the desire to reach some spiritual heights and started worshipping the God wholeheartedly. James too did the same and at last they achieved what they once aspired for. So, see how two absolutely different people with different personas achieved something so extraordinary just because of their tremendous efforts and will power. Hence, concluding, we need to detach ourselves from everything material and non-material too.

So, those who want to achieve something spiritually should first shun the feeling and thought of achieving and then take a step further. One who is spiritually elevated and more liberated as a soul has naught expectations and believes in the oneness of God. When one does daily hard work in a particular direction, one will definitely reach immeasurable heights in that domain whereas if one tries to achieve something with more expectations, it reduces the intensity of focus on that particular thing, with the result it diminishes the chance of actual achievement of that specific destination. Hence, if you too want to achieve, stop thinking of the achieving, rather put all your energy into concrete action. Words will never suffice, thoughts would not help much and expectations often betray, the only thing that proves to be the best friend is your right action done with a right attitude in the right direction and at the right time. The Karmic Theory also says almost the same thing that one should do action only and should not expect something in return and must not think of the destination.

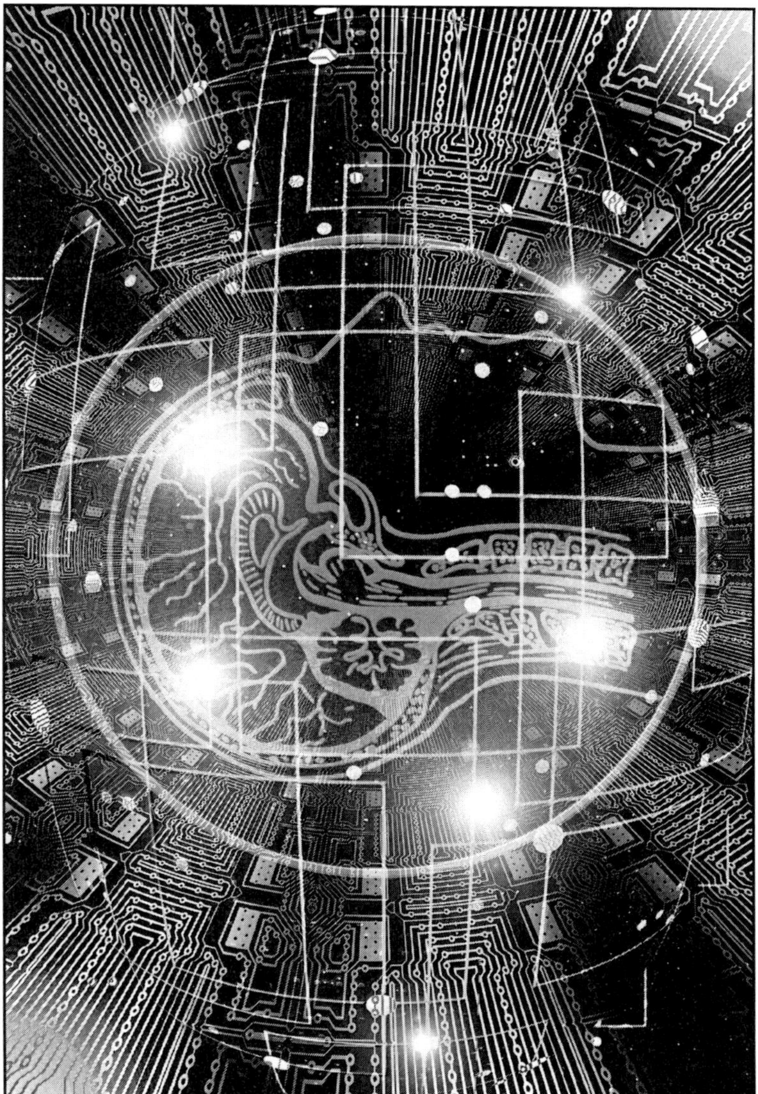

Intellectual Prowess is a wonderful treasure;
It is something; nobody is able to measure;
Failures flee away; sadness departs;
Success is one thing it surely imparts;
About it; you needn't be wary;
With it; happiness you will always carry.

An invaluable asset called Intellectual prowess;
All that it includes; we must possess;
It provides confidence and the right attitude;
This combinedly takes us to the highest altitude;
We feel delighted and it improves our gesture;
Towards life and melancholy comes to a closure.

Chapter - 10

The Intellectual Prowess

We must be well equipped when we step into a battleground. Likewise, in the battleground of life, some things must be owned by us in order to come out as a winner. We can clear the tests put to us in life by God with flying colors if we know which weapons suit us best and which weapon should be utilized at what time in a particular situation. Only those things which are our true assets always help us relieve ourselves from the woes of this materialistic world and get rid of all the problems and tensions. Such assets remain with us till the last breath of ours and never let us feel deprived of something valuable. These are worthy things which prevent us from going astray too. They stand by us through the thick and thin of this life and reduce our liabilities towards others.

One such great and irreplaceable asset is intellectual prowess. It is not something everyone possesses. It is something, the seeds of which are ingrained in almost all the persons but one has to develop them by proper care and monitoring at regular intervals of time during the whole lifetime. It is a precious gift given especially to the mankind by the Almighty. If human beings are higher in order as compared to the other creatures, it is chiefly because of the intellectual capacity of man provided to him by the greatest artist of the world. He created the world and while distributing the qualities among every kind of creature, gave intellectual potential to man. And to our despair, he is using this gift of God in most of the negative ways nowadays.

Intellectual prowess is an eternal and priceless gift. It can be utilized not only for the purpose of solving our problems, but it also acts as a troubleshooter in our routine lives. It also acts as a helping hand in many of our other dealings. When one wants to achieve any aim in life be it personal, career related or spiritual, one needs the sufficient strength and if one faces any kind of challenge, be it adaptability, spiritual, professional, or any other, one needs the help of strong mind. Here the intellectual prowess comes into picture. It is such a weapon of our weaponry, using which we can reach unreachable heights.Being the proud owner of wisdom feels good.

The signs of a wise man are that he puts his intellectual prowess to maximum use. It is a boon for the wise and the worthy. Wise, in the real sense of the words and worthy meaning those who deserve such a precious thing as it is. Intellect is often linked with the abstract things of this abstract world, but it has its meaning really embedded in a much deeper layer of human mind which his usual and normal common sense is unable to catch. One thing is clear that with the help of it, one cannot only, either solve mathematical concepts or the problems of life, but can achieve a often dreamt of aim too.

The problem is that the concept of intellectual prowess is often mistaken as intelligence which is a common phenomenon. You need intelligence for all the things which at once strike your mind like the normal activities and you will need real intellectual prowess when faced with some really tough situations or questions. When the limit of the normal intelligence is reached, the beginning of the intellectual prowess is noticed. The thin line demarcating the both has to be clearly drawn and understood by the person in his mind. Only when, one is clear in mind, then he can proceed further. Some very intelligent people also falter in trying circumstances, but one who is adept as using his special intellectual skills, is always a winner.

As it is a treasure for the owner, so it must be preserved too. One must never become overconfident and once one recognizes and starts using his intellectual skills, the other precaution is that as an unused razor becomes useless, in a similar fashion, if not utilized for a long time, the power he has in him gets faded over or becomes blunt. So in a way, it is type of razor capable of cutting off the edges of any difficult or trying situation. It if properly practiced can cut off a problem into pieces.

A person who uses it for spiritual knowledge or power, if once becomes successful, has that much energy and power in him that no ordinary person can face him as such. He gains the abilities to analyze people rightly, gets the power to influence people and above all is nearer to God. Such people are rare as it requires a lot of patience, determination, immeasurable confidence in God and oneself and strength and strong will power. And he too needs a sharp intellect. Although in the beginning, it sounds very weird that intellect is somehow related to spirituality. But once, we analyze the complete scenario keeping the facts in mind, we agree with the fact. And we are not here to swallow this fact but will digest it properly. When in ordinary life, one needs so much intelligence to cope up with the situations, is something extraordinary not essential to lead us to the real light? The answer to the question is, yes. There is something, something very sharp and razor-edged needed to show us the light through the darkness which is also immense.

That power which is within us but is yet to be recognized properly, is yet to be given the proper place in the world is intellectual prowess. And one wonders how the ordinary human mind has not been able to comprehend properly that something extraordinary is always needed to reach the extraordinarily beautiful, the whole, the extraordinarily large; the Divine.

Motivation is the necessary help to friends, in need, if found;
It can also be given, in tough circumstances to those around;
It restores confidence and generates a lot of positive energy;
The result, in true sense, is the required synergy;
Motivation requires a specific set of skills;
It is a matter of learning and few thrills;
The motivated person gets pacification;
The motivator, in turn gets inner satisfaction;
Motivation is a process of providing invisible support;
You provide the necessary help and then depart.

Chapter - 11

Motivational Adventure

How much do you believe in yourself? When you ask this question to yourself, the answer may be affirmative or a negative one. If you believe in yourself, you must believe in the powers within you which are deep seated. Motivation is one of such things which need to be clearly understood and its sources finely demarcated from one another based on certain parameters.

The moment you are faced with a dilemma of any kind or trouble or are indecisive, you seek motivation. The sources from which this motivation can be drawn can be broadly categorized into two types, one which lies outside "Self" and the other which lies within the "Self". The former is seemingly easier to find and you may find many reliable outer sources of motivation. But these sources somewhere keep you aloof from your own powers and slowly make you dependent on such sources forever. If you continue to rely upon others for motivation, you will suffer at the end.

In this slow and destructive process of growing dependence on others, your own negative thinking and lack of confidence in yourself plays the role of a catalyst which makes the whole process fast. You should not be even completely dependent on the Almighty for motivation of any kind as God Himself has given us all the powers to be self-reliant in every manner. There are certain moments which occur in everybody's life when either one cannot think of any outer motivational source or doesn't trust others. Then, the need of the inner motivators which we have been blessed with, by the Supreme Soul arises. These inner motivators cannot be exactly demarcated from one another but have sharp distinction from the outer motivators. Whereas the inner motivators are not only the best and authentic ones, they also complement our inner growth and personality development.

Just like a good and dedicated teacher, who teaches everything to his disciples and withdraws himself in order to allow the growth of his students, inner motivators show us the light to the right path, help us in adversity and then withdraw to allow our growth. Only in this way, you will be able to lead a healthy life. Hence, you should be internally motivated. People who are internally motivated have clearly distinct features from those who depend on external motivation. The personality traits of the two types of men show tremendous variations in the long run.

In case you are looking for a dynamic personality, you will have to go on an adventurous journey. The journey in which there is nobody with you except your inner guiding light. You will travel and may discover some new plateaus, valleys or islands of your mind and heart. It has been called a journey here as one doesn't reach any tangible heights during this but goes through a process of overall progress. You start with a low morale, lessening confidence level, deepening distress and higher amount of stress and finally after the journey find yourself full of confidence, positive outlook and a deadening will power.

This can't be completely achieved in case of people depending on outer motivators. In order to make your adventurous journey of motivation a success, you must indulge inner motivators. In today's world, you may find almost everything with the help of money but the want of a true well-wisher or a person who can motivate you to a high level is always there. What is the reason behind so many people coming under stress or feeling lonely? The answer lies in the fact that people have started depending more on external sources for their inner peace and solutions to problems in life. Nowadays, the masses don't trust themselves; rather they don't trust God completely. We say we believe in God and follow His guidelines. Do we really do so? A big No is the answer. If we would have trusted ourselves, we would not have been in search of others to solve our problems to this extent. And we realize the fact; the first guideline by God to lead life is to "Believe in Yourself", which we all have forgotten decades back.

It is human who has built the supercomputers, it is he who has devised various ways of solving universal problems, it is he who by using his brain can troubleshoot varied things, and he has the most developed learning potential among all the creatures. These human qualities are essentially embedded in all the human beings, some use and develop them; some keep them in a non-functional state. It is really a pity to see that some people depend on others even for trivial matters of their lives. An entity, so strongly built and gifted with such an immeasurable treasure has lost self-confidence.

All these things have a profound link with motivation and the journey of motivation. These are two separate things. Motivation can be drawn for a particular matter or at a particular time, but motivational journey is an adventurous journey during which you learn how to practically implement the things already present in you and you learn to be self-reliant forever. A person, who seeks motivation, may find it easier to depend upon others for the time being, which proves to be detrimental to his growth later on. Whereas a person who is all set to go on an adventurous ride along with the mind, the heart, the soul is sure to achieve the long-term aim of being independent in every respect. Such a person also develops a special bonding with Almighty as he knows that He has gifted us with such a treasure inside and all of us must be grateful to Him.

Hence, if you want to become a dynamic, outgoing, confident and healthy individual, try relying on yourself than on others. Motivation if sought should be sought within than outside. It is the essence of a healthy and prosperous life.

Emotions are such sensuous sensations;
Which create the necessary vibrations.
Without them, we cannot think of actions;
Devoid of them, we cannot imagine reactions;
To them are attached many false notions;
Which create unnecessary imaginations.
In human life, they have carved a niche for themselves;
Without them, there is a void in the rest of ourselves.

Emotions occur in everyone's life without exception;
They are to some extent in a habit of deception;
They are akin to sentiments and feelings;
They are God's most wonderful creations.

Chapter - 12

Crests and Troughs of Emotions

Emotions, something we all know, we all feel, we all respect! They are the fundamentals of life. Without emotions, the expectation of life is baseless. Most of us only feel and respect emotions, don't know them. But is the knowledge required? Is not feeling an emotion the right way of doing justice to it and respecting it? Of Course, it is!

When we feel something and have certain place for it in our lives, we also have to face difficult situations related to it. These are called the challenges associated with it, which are unavoidable. As we have earlier discussed, the emotional challenges are the most important type of challenges that a person face during his lifetime. Unlike other kinds of challenges, emotional challenges cannot be easily identified and have to be dealt with carefully.

If we look at the roots, we will find that it is only highs and lows of emotions that create turbulence in our lives. It happens in everybody's life without exception. The balanced state of anything doesn't create challenges for us but it is the different than the normal state which is a matter of concern. It means, highs and lows or crests and troughs occur in everybody's life, in every plane or sphere. Just the fact which is to be kept in mind is that everything is a challenge but not a trouble or a problem for us.

If the case is of emotions and the challenges related to them, we have to be a bit careful. As we sometimes come to know of these challenges later on and by the time we have become emotionally weak as can be attacked by invaders like emotional breakups, emotional tortures, direct or indirect and so on. All of the above mentioned work faster in a emotionally weak heart. Just like any enemy invades us when we are vulnerable and weak and tries to overpower us. Likewise, wrong notions, feelings of insecurity and loneliness arise in emotionally weak people.

First of all, I would like to condemn the use of phrase emotional wreck in common parlance as there is no such word. I am not at all acquainted with any such phrase. If we already use the most negative possible word for a person or situation, there is no hope left. And above all, this is a hard fact which is beyond every other fact that God has given human beings immense power to face storms and tsunamis of life and emerge a winner. So, right from this moment, we should stop the usage of the phrase, " emotional wreck" for anyone.

If we think we are trapped in a situation, we are and if we think we can fight, we as warriors fight and the outcome is likely to be negative. The fact can be better illustrated by the given example:-

Once upon a time there was a king and he sentenced a person to death for some crime as the king considered him to be guilty of the crime. Then, by luck, the man was asked his last wish and he said that he should be given 6 months time and he will make the king's horse speak like humans. The king laughed and said fine as the king was sure that he would never be able to fulfill his promise and would be killed. But later when asked upon by another man that why he said so, the man replied that nobody was sure of what was going to happen. It might happen that the king would not remain the king in 6 months or might it be that the horse starts speaking like humans! So, if one has positive outlook, one can do anything. Later on, the kingdom was invaded by another king, the previous king was removed and the new king finding the man innocent freed him. Hence, it was the positive outlook and approach towards life which made the man a free soul.

Emotions are invisible but they create visible effects. When we say one is emotional, it is a normal and healthy sign of being human. But getting over emotional over an issue or anything else is not at all a healthy sign, neither is becoming less emotional or emotionless, good for the long run in life.

The emotional imbalances are a result of our negligence towards our personalities. We falter when we don't pay attention to the changing moods, behavioral patterns, attitudes and our growing dependence on our emotions. If we diagnose these in the beginning and try to correct them, we can achieve the tough goal of controlling emotional imbalances. But if we are unable to recognize, in time, the change in moods, fluctuating behavioral patterns, formation of false notions and incorrect attitudes, we are bound to suffer from emotional imbalances.

But again, we need not consider this as a problem. Come on! It's another challenge of life for us. You have to take outside help most of the times when you undergo an emotional change or face an emotional turmoil in life. Emotions make us healthy, emotions make us rich internally. If devoid of emotions, a human is no better than an automatic machine. To make life meaningful and full of colors, we need the spice of emotions in it. If we dissect any emotion, be it anger, fear, love, sympathy, hatred or jealousy, they have their own respective shades which make us complete in the literal sense of the term.

There are certain emotions which have a negative connotation attached to them like hatred, anger, fear, jealousy, and there are certain others which have positive attributes attached to them like love, sympathy, pity, and so on. The emotions with a negative connotation are generally regarded as harmful for the health of the society. Whereas those with positive attributes attached to them are regarded exemplary and are considered to be the signs of a healthy man. But all these well-fed notions are not completely correct.

A person becomes complete only if he moves through the ordeal of life facing all the kinds of emotions. No emotion can be called as a completely negative emotion. It depends on an individual that how he uses the potential of a negatively shaded emotion and channelizes it in the positive direction. A person in anger can be rude or violent and another person may utilize his increased energy level during anger by engaging himself in any sporting activity.

One person can nourish the seeds of hatred to the level that instill poison in relations and another person may try to find out the reason behind the hatred and resolves it by mutual understanding. A person on one hand can be jealous and hamper his own growth and another person on the other hand may try to find out the positive and admirable qualities of the opponent or the competitor and try to develop such qualities in himself. This is called giving the right direction to wrong emotions. Hence, the quality of emotions cannot be defined in black and white.

There is no such emotion which is altogether positive and there exists no such emotion which is totally negatively shaded.

Rather, I would like to use the term" Trying Emotions" for them as under such emotions, we are tried and tested in the difficult odds. If these emotions have no place in our lives or their importance is lessened, we would never be able to find out the weaknesses in ourselves, analyze ourselves and then emerge as a better and stronger being. Emotions which make us rich internally are basically these emotions as they are the ones which lead to the positive emotions or positive traits in our personality later on. They come in us, for a moment, we feel the heat of negativity and insecurity, but soon everything disappears and what remains is a glow of victory- victory over the negative self.

The sun then shines when the new morning dawns with the revelation of a fact that nothing is made up of all good and hence no human being too can be completely termed as good with the entire positive emotions in him. One learns to persevere in odds, so do he learns from the darker side of his, a lot.

Until the time, we are blindly taken on the worldly path unaware of what we have to overcome, what we have to fight with, we have no weapons in the war of life to face the challenges. As soon as we know the enemy residing inside us which we have to over overpower, we are blessed with divine wisdom to convert our negatives into positives, weaknesses into strengths, and we then reach from the land of unknown to the era of the known.

For that we need introspection, deep introspection, which acts as the input for the desired output.

We all are the creations of God and while creating us, He took proper care of all the requisitions of assembling a good creature. He knows which emotion is to be induced in which quantity in a normal human being as some emotions are more powerful and cannot be handled if induced in larger doses in a human being.

Why is there such hue and cry over the topic of emotions in this world? One must take them normally too. We make food, we consume it, work for the day and take rest in the remaining time. It is a normal daily routine. In a similar fashion, we can get emotional over one matter or the other too. It is completely acceptable and tolerable.

The problem arises when we feel over emotional or we express our emotion more frequently. We need to learn to maintain a balance and should know what to express, when to express and where to express. We have to come at good terms with all of them.

The balance in these two poles of human attitude is the topmost priority and requirement. It is mandatory for a healthy living. A balance in the positive and negative emotions is needed. We need not and we cannot delete the negative emotions altogether. Try to remove the word negative from your dictionary. If someone or some challenge or situation or some emotion is tough to you, it is inspiring, and widens our view about that topic. We come to know new things. For, it is just like we have replaced the word problem with challenge; we would have to replace the term negative emotions with trying emotions in our minds. It removes the negative connotation attached to them and reduces half of our burden.

Then whenever a trying emotion comes in our life, we just have to pacify it first and then slowly replace it with a positive or a better one. If we do it consciously in the beginning, later on we get habitual of it.

For example, one day I was getting angry over something, I don't know the idea of my sister came to my mind, whom I love very much.

Suddenly, my anger first got pacified and then got converted into the feeling of love for her and I forgot the matter. Likewise in case if anyone of you gets overpowered by a trying emotion, just pacify yourself a bit or think of someone you love, you will then be out of clutches of that trying emotion. This is a tested method.

So take emotions as your friends rather than as your problems. And help anyone out of an emotional challenge is a great work to do indeed.

Evolve high, liberate yourself;
And come to terms with your 'Self';
Let the soul breathe, let the sun shine;
Let us again drink that old wine;
Of togetherness, solidarity and unity;
The feeling of living in one city;
Let the flowers again aspire;
And the fragrances truly respire;
Let the pastoral feel come to us again;
And the vitality and vigor regain;
Why not enjoy the moonlit night?
And holding pillows again sleep tight;
As if the world is safe and we secure;
It is a beautiful place, much to adore.

Chapter - 13

Restoration of Peace

Peace is something which is an important aspect of the entire universe. Every thing needs to be at peace in order to result into something positive. In this universe, every being and everything tends to follow the law of entropy or increase in disorder in the system. Much of the energy available cannot be utilized constructively for any work in such a scenario.

In order to tap that potential source of energy in a positive manner, one thing needs to be done foremost and that is to try to maintain maximum peace and orderliness in the entire system, i.e., the universe. The universal system and nature has a law that if anything is done with dedicated efforts putting in a lot of energy, then the outcome is usually positive and the challenge ceases to exist. There is then the arrival of a new dawn. This new situation is the much awaited scene which everyone wants. So, bringing about peace, harmony and orderliness is the aim which we need to achieve.

It needs to be done at two levels, the personal or the inner level and the interpersonal or the outer level.

At the personal or the inner level, peace is very important. It means harmony with oneself or the inner self. A person who is at harmony with himself reflects his inner beauty and confidence and is on his way of success in his respective field of activity. Exuberance is that quality which comes from within and is closely related to inner peace. The person who is at peace with himself is usually at peace with his surroundings and others. It creates an atmosphere of mutual harmony and trust among living beings.

Thus, peace at inner level is the first and the foremost requisite for an overall peaceful society. Tranquility within is achieved by various measures such as practicing meditation, developing an optimistic attitude towards life, analyzing our weak characteristics and replacing them with stronger and better ones, striving for perfection in one's sphere by the way of perseverance and determination, inculcating the habit of concentrating properly on things, and by taking a pledge to work for the betterment of society.

All these things are mandatory for a good and peaceful living. The habit of practicing meditation keeps you closer to the Divine and hence takes you away from materialistic considerations. It helps you in reaching a higher level of consciousness where trivial matters of life don't exist and where all the differences of mine and thine have vanished. Most of the clashes in human life arise due to a false sense of possession which is baseless. We fight for that which was never ours, which is not ours and which will never be ours. As this whole world is made by God and everything, big or small, animate or inanimate, good or bad belongs to Him. He is The Creator of this wonderland called universe. So, after reaching higher levels of consciousness, we explore new horizons where there is light of wisdom and tranquility leaving behind no space for darkness of ignorance.

Developing a positive attitude is helpful in our long journey of life as it accelerates our pace towards our goals and leaves little space for any distractions. By the time, we are covered by a blanket of pessimistic attitude; everything seems to create trouble for us and restricts us to narrow thinking too. Weird ways start coming to our minds for fighting against the challenges of life which lead us nowhere. The reason behind this is that if we don't see the shine of positivism, we move our hands in darkness and as a result are not in harmony with ourselves. But soon, there comes the sunlight, bringing positive attitude into our lives which almost culminates all our troubles landing us into a land of peace. It fills our heart with reverence. It provides us self-confidence. All the barriers between us and peace are now demolished and we can easily taste the flavor of tranquility and feel the fragrance of love around.

Our analysis of our weaknesses and their conversion into strengths leads us towards the appropriate way of life and gives us a higher place in life because such a human being can rightly be called as evolved. Those who remain in the same condition for the whole of their lives in which they are, are the ones who have not made enough efforts to analyze themselves. They don't rise above a certain level as a human being. Once you rise above that level, you realize the difference between the right and the wrong doings. Thereafter, you will not do anything to hurt others or there are lesser chances of the arousal of any chaotic situation. Peace is thus imparted first at inner level then reaches at the interpersonal level.

If one strives for perfection in a specific sphere of life, then he concentrates upon one thing and does not delve into other areas much. This also reduces the chances of any kind of conflict. Although these two seem to be unrelated things, they are one. The more you concentrate upon your own goal and strive for perfection in work, the more you go away from unnecessary things which create conflicts. This is an easy method, the application of which brings you closer to peace.

If every one of us takes an easy pledge to work for the betterment of the society, almost 90% of our goal is reached and peace is attained at all levels. Such a pledge not only makes us a better human being but renders us the ability to feel empathetically for others. We see the problems in lives of others with their eyes and this leads to demolition of narrow barriers of selfish interests in society. All this eventually leads to a tranquil atmosphere all around.

Restoration of peace at all levels depends much on our efforts and we must realize that we are endowed with the gift of this beautiful universe and must conserve it by all possible means peacefully. If we practice peaceful thinking and peaceful living, we would never have to lose our precious relationships either with our own Self or with our fellow beings.

Conflicts are natural aspects,
Never conceal, regarding them any facts.
Otherwise, they are hard to resolve,
They are not the puzzle you cannot solve.
They are the automatic reactions,
Of our mishandled tasks and actions.
Wrong attitude may sometimes lead to them,
It may cause an overall mayhem
If conflicts are clouding your brain,
Use patience & inner strength to get over the strain.

Conflicts are of two varieties,
Inner and outer conflicts are there to cause ambiguities.
Outer conflicts can be resolved by mutual talks,
Inner conflicts need centralized lonely walks.
Outer conflicts are very obvious,
Inner conflicts are somewhat vicious.
Both create uneven terrain in your life,
They are like unwanted rains, may be of any type.
You are wet outside with heavy waters,
You are thirsty inside and nothing caters.
To your need at the time of need,
But self-confidence will do indeed.
Just strongly hold your hand in yours,
Sometimes, you have to wipe your own tears.

Chapter - 14

Inner and Outer Conflicts

Conflict, though the word may not sound so pleasing, yet it is an important aspect of everyone's life. Conflicts may arise out of any circumstance and due to a number of reasons. But it never means that beyond a conflict, there lie disrupted threads of relations or spoiled terms. However, one must master the art of resolving conflicts with tact and care.

Conflicts are erroneously taken as misunderstanding creating agents, though they deliver good returns at times too. Let us take a fresh look at conflicts with this example:-

Example (i):- Peter and Rose were in a soulful relationship of husband and wife. Two years passed and both were leading a romantic and satisfactory life together. They were so used to each other that one could not spend more than an hour without the other. If they had to be away from each other, they made it a point to talk regularly.

One silly morning, they woke up and argued over a petty issue and later almost fought over it. They decided not to talk to each other. The fight suddenly became so big that their egos intervened and they didn't even dine together. Three days were gone like this and the misunderstanding continued. One day Peter decided to resolve the conflict by sitting and coming up with a mutually agreeable solution. When both had a hour full of discussion, they were tired and Peter was thirsty. Rose suddenly went up and brought a glass of water for him. At that moment, just by holding Rose's arm, Peter said, "See,

Dear how much you care for me and love me?" "Is the issue bigger than our love or are our egos so great that we simply can ignore the deep love behind the sustenance of our relation and let the petty issue rule our hearts?"

This was exactly what Rose was thinking about. She held his arm and said that she also wanted to end the fight there. Both had a hearty laugh at the end and hugged each other. Never again in life they had such a long fight. They had conflicts, but only those which created more love between them than ever before. Both of them had learnt an art, the art of resolving conflicts in a productive way.

As is clear from this example, man can harness any situation into a productive one. The more negative a situation seems to be, the more productive, it may become. Similarly any kind of conflict can be resolved and the resulting scenario may be a better one than the previous one.

Conflicts, today, seem to be an everyday affair. Anywhere you go, you can find them looking straight at your face as if they are challenging you to try to resolve them. Not every time you should accept the challenge. As there are certain conflicts which are resolved only with the assistance of an outside authority.

So, how do you decide which conflict to face head-on and which not? Who tells you the way to resolve them? And another obvious question that comes in our minds is about the type of conflicts.

Conflicts basically, are of two strains, inner and outer. Outer conflicts as the name suggests are more apparent than the inner conflicts. If there is a conflict between two people, it can be easily recognized whereas the conflict inside the mind or heart of a person is not easily recognizable. Both the types of conflicts cause disturbance but the type and degree of disturbance caused varies in both the cases.

Outer conflicts can be of various types like conflict between siblings, conflict between life-partners, between relatives, between employee and employer, between two members or groups of society, between friends, and so on. The number of conflicts that exist in this world is directly proportional to the number of relations that exist in the world.

On the one hand, these conflicts whether personal or professional or social can be resolved by the mutual talks of the persons involved; on the other hand if the situation worsens, an outside authority may be needed to intervene. This is nothing new I am offering you, but it is explained here just to remind that if efforts are made to resolve a conflict, first people involved must try to resolve it themselves.

We are not much concerned here about the outer conflicts that arise due to various situations but they play a vital role in determining our inner peace too. In every situation, one should consider the fact that the behavior of the other person is bad or his attitude is different from yours due to difference of opinions. There is nothing in this world that cannot be resolved with patience and self-controlled talks and behavior. There are basically two types of people: those who lose their temper in the event of a conflict and those who maintain their calm and poise even under extreme situations. It always depends upon you to decide which type of personality you want to develop.

No one is absolutely good or bad in this world. No one is perfect. We are humans and it is the reason behind our imperfections. If we always keep this thing in our mind, we will easily forgive people and thereby easily forget bad experiences. We all make errors, commit mistakes, and are bad to someone or the other sometime or the other. But at the time of most conflicts that occur, we easily overlook our mistakes and see the mistakes done by others. It is the only reason of the rise of a conflict.

If someone has said that it is better to forgive others easily and forget their mistakes, it is not for their benefit, it is beneficial for us. It helps to maintain our internal peace and harmony even in difficult times. That inner peace is the only weapon, which then is used by us to resolve our inner conflicts. So, the thing which is endangered today in the world is not only wild-life or flora but also inner peace. It has become such a valuable thing that is in dearth nowadays.

If any time inner conflict arises, there are reasons behind it. The primary reason is the dissatisfaction that exists in our mind and heart which maybe further due to various reasons. Dissatisfaction that arises in mind can be removed only with spiritual bonding with God. If we concentrate on the Almighty, we will find that He has blessed us with a mighty nature and a wonderful universe. We will soon forget the thing which we could not get or could not achieve and will rely on God for all our answers. In fact, all the things which no one can explain are explained by concentrating inwards and through introspection. There is no better a way than focusing on God, an authority outside this world. If we keep on revolving our mind around the materialistic aspects and if our heart keeps on disturbing us by wanting the pleasures of the world, we will never be able to come out of that circular trap of desires. We have to shun all the desires for sometime and feel what the nature wants us to feel.

Our problems and their solutions lie within us and thus I call it a challenge to find the solution from within. I will not spoon-feed you regarding each step of remembering God otherwise that would be stupid enough of me. Everyone who believes in God has a different method of reaching Him, some talk to God in loneliness, some meditate, some chant prayers and hymns while some other find solace in the lap of nature. It varies from individual to individual.

Another thing of utmost importance is patience. If we have patience, most of the troubles are solved with the passage of time. Life is valuable and nothing is more valuable than life itself. So instead of giving room to any conflict in our life, we must move towards a peaceful life.

is impaired in people who always think of themselves. One should neither be an altruist nor an extremely selfish creature. The world runs on the basis of social interactions and no one can live alone. Hence one has to think of others too before taking any step that may affect people at large.

One should care for oneself and try to fulfill all the dreams and desires. But such a person cannot be called selfish; rather he can be regarded as aware. Selfish people not only think of themselves but can do any work of their interest even at the cost of others. This impairs their broad vision and inculcates the habit of thinking narrowly most of the time. So a broad-minded, aware and sensible human being is the need of today's world. If every person works towards developing a balanced persona, then there would be lesser worries and more happiness in the world.

We all must strive to achieve the target of making the world a better, happier, more prosperous and a more peaceful place to live in. This end is far from us but is not unachievable.

The bigger question is of keeping a check on our negative tendencies. If we keep on accepting every demand of our mind or heart , then negative shades appear in our habits resulting in varied disoriented behavioral patterns. The brain is the controlling center of the human body but it in turn should be under proper control of our whole personality. The brain should guide us towards the best feasible path or alternative and lreave the rest on us. Heart is governed by passions, desires, attractions, emotions and intuitions. Hence, while taking the important decisions of life, the heart must convey the signals to the brain, the brain must analyze and then send message via message impulses. When the heart and the brain do not coordinate, the brain should supersede.

Oh Man! O Man! What all do you finally need?
What is your true craving, what is your greed?
For what have you landed on this planet Earth?
What is still left in life, of which there is dearth?
What are your worries and what are your answers?
To the questions about life which really bothers.
You are made of flesh, bones and blood;
Of souls like you, there exists a flood.
To be one with the divine, to feel Him and co-exist;
You must follow the path of salvation and persist.
Rise above your own self and break your sphere;
To selfless existence and altruism, you must adhere.
You live life your way, there is no harm;
Without tranquility and divine connectivity, exists no charm.

Chapter - 16

The Salvation

Salvation, a word that itself if spoken, creates a positive impact on one's mind. Salvation cannot be accomplished within one life even. But one can make a step towards achieving salvation in the present life itself. We can devote some of our time to things related to God, spirituality or either we can devote ourselves to the help of the needy. These are two ways which can take us on the path of salvation. We are given one life and the one who makes the best use of it reaches directly to God's heart.

Yes, salvation may definitely be achieved by living in this physical world and by leading a normal life. We must be aware of the problems and challenges that surround the world and must contribute our little bit towards helping others. Devoting some part of our lives to someone means fulfilling our primary duty towards God. Moreover, you gain immense satisfaction and inner tranquility in return.

Why do we work? Why do we eat? Why do we enjoy life? Why do we go to spiritual teachers and people who can pacify us? The answers to all these questions lie in the fact that we all need a basic thing- peace & satisfaction. And this cannot be achieved with the sole aim of satisfying our own needs. We will have to go out and search for our answers ourselves. We will have to make an effort to decrease the misery in this world. If you make an effort to lessen other's pain, God relieves you of your own pain in the longer run.

Salvation is the method, the path not the aim. The main aim of humanity is to reach God. We all are in search of the Supreme Soul and we all are bound to one only.

A person living in his house carrying normal routine activities, along with taking care of his personal and professional needs may be the one who has attained salvation or who has experienced it. On the other hand, a saintly figure always occupied with the work of God, in the chanting of His name, performing religious and spiritual practices may not have attained salvation in any sense or in the true sense.

It is something which starts from devotion, purity of heart, soul and thoughts and reaches the Divine, the Supreme Soul. The prayers expected always are not the ones which are said with loud voice, tough mantras, religious functions or even spiritual practices. The prayers heard, valued and accepted are mostly the ones which are silent, deep hearted, pure, innocent and for the benefit of all. There are people in this world who seldom ask anything to God for them but always try to pray for others, related or unrelated to them. Such prayers have a far greater probability of reaching Almighty and getting accepted.

That is why it is sometimes said that always pray for the good of others and God will take care of you. Despite knowing this fact, one should selflessly pray for those for whom he cannot do any service and do service of those whom he can render service to. One must help others on all small and big occasions wherever feasible and extend one's personal boundaries even to help. Helping others should run in your veins like bloodstream.

I know the question arising in your mind is that nowadays those who help others are considered to be foolish and less worthy and sometimes people call them by names like stupid, half-minded, etc. But you have to keep one thing in mind that all good causes have to be performed without expectations and the end result should be left in the hands of God.

Salvation is not only being one with God, but also about the immense satisfaction, joy, and peace you experience even amidst the turmoil of situations.

In today's worldly sphere of worries and calamities, what we need utmost is peace for all. If we begin at our personal level and succeed, then this can reach others too. One person can guide others and so on. Salvation is neither a strategy nor the aim, it is the path to the ultimate divine peace.

See the universe and the skies,
See the lows and the highs,
See the beautiful blooming flowers,
See the evergreen trees and water showers,
Hear the chirping of the birds,
Notice the huge cattle herds,
Little blooming faces of tiny tots,
Notice the variance of masses in lots,
The grace of the valleys and the mountains
The noise of the springs and fountains,
The innumerable stars at night
The rainbow and its beautiful sight,
All has been the gift of a universal creation,
God is the creator who created such variance.

Chapter - 17

Creativity and the Creator

Creation is something universal. We all are creations of God and this whole universe is again a creation of Him. Somebody who creates something has been defined as a creator. There are several reasons behind different creations but the underlying fact is the same. The one who is gifted with the power of innovation and creative ideas will get satisfaction only through his creation.

Not many people have the power to create something new but many others have the desire of being creative. Can one develop creativity? Is creativity a God gifted attribute or itself a created quality? Though most of the people who have created great things like books, satellites, rockets, paintings, music, dance forms, any many other inventions were god-gifted with an insight to creativity. But this cannot be ruled out that if one has innovative ideas, then they can be easily converted into productive and wondrous creations.

The gain from creative pursuits is immense and immeasurable as the person gains not only in terms of personal satisfaction but is also able to develop a better personality with a better and positive attitude and outlook towards life and varied phenomenon related to the universe. He who created the world also created people with the inbuilt ability to create even better than Him. He has rendered all his creative powers to such people who in turn utilize it in making new things and exploring new dimensions of life and death.

One if wants to be spiritual and near to God must be creative. Moreover creativity brings our inner self to light and remove darkness of self ignorance from our lives.

Every day we should ask a question to ourselves, "Have we contributed something good or great to our lives yesterday?" "Have we been able to change the situations of our lives and the lives of those around us towards positivity?"

Believe me the answer to these questions are the driving force to creative pursuit in the lives of those who have till date not explored the creativity zone of their lives. As whenever we want to contribute something new to lives, we need a changing factor which only something innovative, something creative, something new can provide. Likewise, when we want to change an existing situation of our or our near and dear ones' lives, radically, we need a motivational yet creative idea or pursuit. Hence, creativity moves our lives on the path of positive change in the third gear.

Being a creator is a matter of bliss. You may be a cook, a potter, a painter, a dramatist, a musician, a teacher, a scientist, an engineer, a doctor, or in any other profession with a creative or innovative bent of mindset. If you feel reluctant to new things, you may waste your all good and higher studies and if your mind is on an exploring voyage, you may change the world around you with your new inventions or creations.

Not necessarily, the solution to all the problems, be it inner and outer conflicts, conflicting egos, managing environmental issues, societal upheavals, lies in creating in something new or finding the hidden creator in yourself. But, yes, it is a pathway! A pathway to find out that aspect of yourself, which you could not explore due to worldly hesitations, self-made restrictions, weakness of heart, blockages of mind, societal obstacles.

Creativity is a pathway which will show a new light to you, which will make you realize your real worth, which will bring intense cheer to your soul along with peace to heart and a sense of achievement to your mind. The matter is all connected with the tri-sensitivity zone, the mind, the heart and the soul. Once, all the three feel satisfied, fulfilled and have their complete share, all is well with the life and psyche.

O Dear Soul, the path of life and the beyond is not always even;
Obstacles and conflicting terrains will come which may be uneven.
The easy path is just our brain-child and life's unreal perception;
The rough way is the one to be pursued to avoid deception.
Avoidance and ignorance of hurdles is not the correct strategy;
Combatting the odds with full guts will solve life's analogy.
Knowing your weaknesses is the most powerful weapon;
Avenues to improve and strengthen yourself, it will open.
Understanding the obstacle's nature and kind is a must;
Then evaluating all your strengths is needed and just.
Then locate the points of access of the hurdle in your lives;
Only then all the deterrent arms of the danger will come out of hives.
Strengthening all your strengths with integrity comes the next;
This action will determinate the intensity of your win and will text;
The command to your brain to use the strengths when & where;
Else all the strategies formulated & plans will scatter here & there.
Keeping yourself locked from all nook & corners is not needed;
You must come out and face the situation as it is seeded.
The moment which brings the fear of the outcome in your mind;
Will devastate all the work & actions will be taken like being blind.
Have the courage in your heart and trust in yourself all the time;
After combatting all the odds, your belief in the Thine' will also shine.

Chapter - 18

Combatting the Odds

Life is a treasure to cherish but often we miss this wonderful opportunity due to odds in our lives. What are these odds? How do they affect our lives? How can we combat them? Where do they generate from? What are the strengths and weaknesses of these odds which can be utilized to defeat them? All of these are valid questions which arise in our minds and if not, they should.

The odds may be of several kinds viz. the ever-changing scenarios of life related to people, institutions, relationships, attitudes, preferences, priorities, short term and long term goals of life, stress created due to varied reasons, inability to express, under-estimation of self by others, degrading self-worth due to low self-confidence, ignorance about situations, hurt self-esteem, varying moods, harm due to underemployment or unemployment, inability to pursue studies of own choice, odds of married life like incompatibility amongst life-partners, non-expression of real feelings, mental and physical tortures of one or the other, adjustment and adaptability problems, ageing odds such as understanding differences amongst near ones, devaluation by the society, health issues, boredom, loneliness in case of being single or left single due to destiny, unacceptability of the generation gap between the self and the younger members of the family, and many of such kinds.

These odds whether of any kind affect our lives in varied ways. On the first instance, it seems they may harm us, reduce our confidence level, may pose as a danger or act as an obstacle in the path of our success, may demean our values and may wreck our faith in the Divine. But truly speaking, odds are the backbones of our lives. Whether they are small odds or greater challenges, they make us strong.

Odds and adversity is one and the same thing. It is aptly said that adversity is the greatest teacher. They teach those valuable lessons and of life to us which are never being taught in any class of the whole world. They teach us how to live life with caution and we must keep a support system always ready for any emergency scenario. The odds come with a gloomy side attached to them but when they depart they leave us with a feeling of enhanced confidence, victory over our own weaknesses and fears, a much greater understanding of the self, the world and the strategies to be adopted in future for larger odds to come.

They are our helping hands. Odds are our hidden true friends in this world full of deceit and hatred. Just like every coin has two sides, odds are two-sided. They challenge our might to face and defeat them and at the same instance, they give us an opportunity to win over our weak points, convert them into our plus points which will protect and strengthen us always.

They give us an opportunity to learn and grow at their cost. When you face an odd, everyone will believe as you are suffering from an odd, hence your capabilities and potentials may not have been harnessed to the greatest extent, thus you get the benefit of the situation. Such a situation gives you ample opportunity to learn & grow. The odds really nurture our self-esteem after our victory over them; they enhance our knowledge and experience in both the situations whether we overcome or combat them or succumb to them.

We can definitely combat these odds by our timely wisdom and appropriate usage of time, space, capital, our strengths like correct attitude, right perception, applying one strategy at a time, and much more. Whenever an odd arrives in your life, do not ignore or neglect it. Analyzing, evaluating, assessing, and understanding an enemy, like an odd is the most important task and the primary thing to do in such cases.

Once you get to know the nature of the odd, its intensity, the damage it can do to your life and comfort, you have to adopt precautions. Devote more of your valuable time in nourishing yourself, like reading books, gaining knowledge even about the things related to that odd situation, meditating, relaxing in your own ways and by all these means your mind, body and soul will come to an interconnected and relaxed state.

Then strengthen your weak points. For example, you are a student and the physics exam is nearby. The problem is that you have not practiced enough to get good marks in it. You have completed the theory portion but practical portion is still posing a problem for you. What you will do except being perplexed and worried is that firstly strengthen your weak point, the practical or numerical part in the time available. Moreover, without wasting much time on that you will have to revise the theory portion too, and that is already your strong point. With the application of this strategy you will score well in your exam with the help of combined marks of theory and numerical portion.

During any examination of life, if you get perplexed and nervous, you are half-defeated. In many big interviews all over the world, the interviewers judge the confidence level of the interviewees.

These odds are generated by life-cycle or the cycle of time standardized for each and every person. Every person faces different odds in his lifetime than the other. These odds are generated as per our fears, our weaknesses and also to test our greatest strengths. What we fear often poses as a challenge or as an odd in our lives. The greatest odds of our lives are those in front of which we feel weak as they demand those qualities for fighting with them which we lack in or which are our weak points. The other category of odds relate to our strengths. This is the most dangerous ones as being over-confident of our strengths; we take them lightly and get done over. These odds are so generated so as to make us realize our weaknesses and fears and finally to help us get rid of them.

There are strengths and weaknesses of these odds themselves knowing which we will be helped out. Any danger is a danger till you treat it like that. All the odds have a primary psychological effect on us and try to capture and attack our minds first. So, we must not become mental captives of them. Every odd has the strongest effect when we feel over-confident, then it harms the most. We are strong and that is a positive sign but channelizing it properly is a must. Odds terrify us by making us realize that we are weak and attack our fears. We should not become victims of our own fears and weaknesses.

Prior the entry of any odd in our lives, we must try to remove most of our weaknesses and overcome all our fears. Then beyond this the sun shines for us and the moon soothes our soul only. Then there is nothing left to be worried about.

Survival Mind
valuable
productive
admired
worthy
significant
respected
worthwhile
liked
accepted
connected
welcome
included
popular
involved
strong
powerful
certain
protected
tough
secure
safe
helpless
unprotected
insecure
powerless
impotent
defenseless
weak
exposed
left out
excluded
avoided
abandoned
rejected
invisible
alone
discarded
forsaken
despised
disposable
unimportant
insignificant
worthless
inferior
irrelevant

A man can make enemies, he can win friends;
It all depends upon his attitude decided by his ego trends.
Ego of a person is a healthy sign if used appropriately with caution;
Else whole life can be spent with negative ego and the wrong notion.
All have four ego states; Id, Child Ego, Adult Ego and Parent ego;
We must learn more to adjust, adapt, and change and to let go.
Ego is a concept of the mind, unseen and unheard by the others;
Sometimes it creates a difficult sphere around and only bothers.
What we think of our attributes and strengths is self-concept;
It is related to our positive ego state and is easy to accept.
Negative ego state enters when we are bound to narrow vision;
It captures our healthy mindset and keeps us in such a prison;
Where we treat every different view of ourselves as wrong;
We become captives of a single-sided view-point of life and world;
We need nurturing by a healthy, positive, broad mind & its hold.
We need to pamper our egos to boost our self-confidence;
But must monitor and control, on those egos, over-reliance.
We all should take care of our egos and see till they do good;
A person with a positive ego state can move with a raised hood.
Ego if dealt with carefully can save relationships and partnerships;
Ego if goes over the head can destroy even diplomatic relationships.

Chapter - 19

Proper Positioning of Ego in Life

Life gives us ways to express ourselves, whether positively or negatively, which in turn depends on people and situations, but in fact actually on us. Life never expects us to be hostile to anyone just because he or she holds a different view-point, a different opinion from us.

Rather life is a great teacher which always motivates us to be patient with others, to use our logic before our senseless emotions which may be abrupt reactors. Life always makes bus more positive, more docile, more humble, more self-reliant, and more human than before. It is we, who always try to find out deficiencies in things, situations, people and relations. This fault-finding tendency is sometimes lethal. Moreover, we human beings are naturally good at heart, almost all of us, but as soon as we come in contact with others, we start learning from them. Every individual has separate life living tendency and has different way of expression of the same emotions too.

In this way, often other people say something to us or react on our some statement which may be intensely related to our lives, in such a manner that may hurt us. That manner may be just awful or stupid at times, or jovial, still it may hurt us deeply.

Here, originates the concept of EGO. Then we say that our egos were affected. We are ego-hurt at those moments. In such ego-hurt moments, we do not listen to any sensible advice and neither are we ourselves logical.

Ego is a concept of the mind, usually the illogical mind. It is like that naughty child, who if not tamed, will play with our lives throughout.

A person's ego is acceptable and correct to the extent till it reminds him of his actual good qualities, provides the right direction to his life, guides him in all the practical concerns, saves his self-esteem from hurt and deterioration, and teaches adaptability and sensibility and helps him learn from situations and understands people.

Usually a slight negative connotation is attached to the word ego which is highly harmful for everyone and it hinders the real understanding of the term, "Ego".

Ego is not the other name for over-confidence or showing off superiority complex, rather it is a simple attribute which makes this journey of life easy if understood rightly and if correctly used. It can make the terrain of life rough too if based on false ego, we make distances with people and in relationships.

There is a short phrase called ego-centric. What is being meant by an ego-centric individual? Certain people have a limited sphere, a very small domain for people and things in their lives. They do not easily include others in their lives, perhaps due to hesitation and underestimation of the self. Often, what we see, hear and understand depends on our worldly knowledge. We refuse to accept things that are less apparent, implicit and under shadows.

Similarly, these ego-centric individuals have a mindset of their own; they are sometimes diffident type of people, and sometimes the ones who are suffering from inferiority complex. They do not want others to explore their lack in life, and hence make a tight cocoon around them so that none shall enter.

We should thrive on sound bases of docility, humility, self-esteem, self-confidence, fire to succeed, desire to improve, longing for spiritual heights, openness to all scenarios, adjustability to varied conditions, correct perceptions, being judgmental when needed, being strong when required, awareness of our weaknesses, learning capacities enough transparent to learn from our past, mistakes, experiences, people and life, ability to cope with fear, darkness within, and with grief when it arrives, balanced attitude towards happiness, success, relationships, and natural laws.

There is none in this world who would advocate that our lives should be based on mere egos. Ego is a concept of the mind, as already said. It is like a helping hand at times but not the articulator of our faiths and belief-system.

A man with a balanced approach towards life and the one with a perfect blend of balanced head and peaceful heart succeeds in achieving solace even in this packed up world. He gets peace even amidst noises, time for the self even amongst busy schedules, love even in few relations, friendship even from the enemies, company of the divine even while alone and spiritual heights even while performing all worldly duties.

Knowing your inner self is a desire and an important aim;
Be it the shining part or the dark side, there should be no shame.
What we think of ourselves decide things of important nature;
We all are though worthy beings and none is a useless creature.
We have to be correct and precise in weighing our attributes;
We cannot choose only strengths and ignore flaws as it suits.
Self-concept if correct is of great help and nurtures the being;
Timely revision of our views of the self is an in indispensable thing;
To older version of self-concept which is deceptive, we must not cling.
Self-concept should be analyzed and revised as only gain it will bring.
Self-concept has four sides too, which tell us of various shades;
First is what we know of ourselves, and it opens new ways.
Second is what others think of us and we also know those facts;
Third is hidden side which only others know and can be used as tacts.
Fourth is what we and others don't know about our personality;
When this side is revealed, it may throw surprise, sadness or gaiety.
Our Self-concept is made of our own views and others' opinions of us;
We may find it necessary to open up and to improve, discuss.
About our weaknesses and ways to better our whole perspective;
We must take care whom to talk to and be very selective.

Chapter - 20

Self Concept - A Healthy Mental Food

Self-concept is the view or concept we have of ourselves. Everyone makes his view of himself as an individual based on two things, one the opinion of others about him and another, the opinion he holds for himself.

Sometimes the first factor: opinions and views of others regarding the self proves dangerous for many people, as it is true that many a times the opinions and views which others reveal about us are prejudiced, biased and sometimes purposefully made weird or piercing in nature so as to harm one's growth.

The purpose of me writing this chapter is to warn you all who want to truly succeed in their lives based on goodness and humanity to be aware of such negative elements of the society. Just as we cannot separate thorns from a rose flower without which its identity cannot be imagined, we cannot weed out such negative or harmful minded people from the society. What we have to is to be alert enough and to filter every comment or opinion thrown on us. I have used the word, "thrown" as most of the opinions are thrown upon us.

Many people have inculcated a habit of giving advice for free, without asking. Such people have a self-concept according to which they have the answer to most of the queries of the world, they have great bank of wisdom which they can distribute too, and that they are the last resort for resolution of problems of many people who cannot approach anybody beyond them.

The world is full of people who have a discouraging tendency rather than an encouraging one, who have a demotivating attitude rather than a motivating one, who know very well how to let down people rather than to appreciate their real qualities, who value materialistic pursuits more than any intangible attribute of human nature, who know how to exploit people and things but do not understand the value of human qualities like humility, generosity, helpful nature, depth, love, care, wisdom and others. They consider their own mind to be superior to others.

In reality, such people are to be pitied as they have not attained that level of awareness, understanding and depth which is required before entering another man's sphere.

Thus, we must feed ourselves with positive thoughts about ourselves, new ideas, innovative thinking, and healthy attitude. We must enrich a balanced outlook of the world, critical analytical capability for understanding our weak points, and must also develop strong and unbiased decision making capability.

Once a being is surrounded with such petals of positive aura around it, it deciphers the fragrance of oneness. A man who is enlightened can spread light and hence it becomes quintessential to have a healthy mental food on a regular basis. The self-concept is one way of feeding our mind with all the ingredients in correct proportion, be it new ideas, collectivity of thoughts, clear vision, positive attitude, spiritual appetite, divine search, transcendence from the hollow to the complete, beginning of the new journey from the being to the formless, from the minute to the whole, from the senses to the vivid, from the noise to tranquility, from the rage to calmness, from the words to thoughts to vision.

To become such a being, you have to make small start by ignoring unnecessary words that may hamper your inner growth. You have to bypass certain weird comments that may stop you flower. You have to reject some unwanted advice internally that does not suit your own choice of life. The moment you start adopting these small steps, you start growing, becoming more confident, less confused, more patient, more balanced and above all, more happy.

The second step starts with avoiding negative vibrations about other people and things. When your mind is preoccupied with negative things like negative thoughts, vibrations, you cannot progress. The progress of person grows like a perpendicular tree which has strong roots of strong morals and values, which has strong shoots of generosity, humanity, honesty, love, care, charity but still it does not deflect anywhere in its lifetime. Such a tree never attaches itself to the other tree either positively or negatively. Similarly, you have to tread your own path of life ignoring the negativity of life. At the same time, you should not be more attached to anyone so that the attachment becomes an obstacle of your life's path.

As we all have different life paths, different energy levels, different personalities, so we should choose our destination accordingly. We must keep in mind that the feed we give to our mind is the basis of outcome of life.

The journey was long and we chatted much;
You came to know me and I came to know you as such.
From the puzzles of life, we learnt how to manage little strife;
Then we learnt the types and how to deal with the challenges of life.
Then came the burning topic of materialistic tendency and desire;
It should be understood deeply else wrong notions may catch fire.
Spirituality and religion were discussed in depth and caught our eye;
Less knowledge & ignorance of both may create hue and cry.
We learnt how to devise the solutions of challenges from the self;
It was emphasized to empower the power within than to take help.
How nicely we felt the need to develop and enrich the inner zeal;
It is needed to refresh, motivate, empower, & for soul to heal.
We learnt how to attain in life, a particular spiritual altitude;
It takes us beyond the sphere of daily life and changes our attitude.
All possess talent but few are able to unlock their intellectual prowess;
They should harness their capability which is a gift they possess.
Life is nothing but a motivational adventure which takes us ahead;
We should be more self-reliant and move with raised head.
Crests and troughs of emotions come along with life's every phase;
One must know balancing and understanding & avoid illusionary chase.
Inside us lies a huge world which needs restoration of peace;
After its achievement, we feel blessed, light and live with grace.
Inner and outer conflicts are shades of every being's personality;
Dealing with the former one is tougher and this is the basic reality.
We reside in hives of selfish motives which must be captivated;
After uplifting the soul beyond desires, spiritual center is activated.
We all know one goal of human life which is salvation;
You can achieve it while smiling, loving, and caring like any creation.
Arise and develop the spirit of creativity & innovation inside;
You will be flowered, rejuvenated & world will discover your new side.
Combatting the odds of life is no less than fighting a battle unarmed;

Strengthen yourself, remove flaws remain alert, not to be harmed.
Ego, a sensitive weapon, the proper positioning of which in life is must.
Must take care of self-esteem, but be humble to win other's trust.
Self-concept can prove to be a healthy mental food for all and sundry;
Never demotivate yourself or make false concept in a moment's hurry.
I hope all will take care as all of you are important creatures,
Each one is unique with different emotions & features.